CHRISTIAN ENCOUNTERS

SAINT
PATRICK

CHRISTIAN ENCOUNTERS

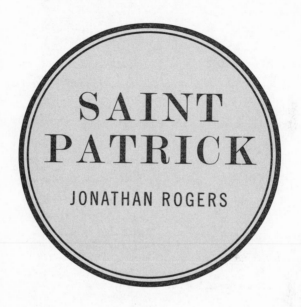

SAINT
PATRICK

JONATHAN ROGERS

THOMAS NELSON
Since 1798

NASHVILLE   DALLAS   MEXICO CITY   RIO DE JANEIRO

Published in Nashville, Tennessee, by Thomas Nelson. Thomas Nelson is a registered trademark of Thomas Nelson, Inc.

Published in association with Eames Literary Service, LLC, Nashville, Tennessee.

Thomas Nelson, Inc., titles may be purchased in bulk for educational, business, fund-raising, or sales promotional use. For information, please e-mail SpecialMarkets@ThomasNelson.com.

Unless otherwise indicated, Scripture quotations are taken from the HOLY BIBLE: NEW INTERNATIONAL VERSION®. © 1973, 1978, 1984 by International Bible Society. Used by permission of Zondervan Publishing House. All rights reserved.

Scriptures marked ESV are taken from THE ENGLISH STANDARD VERSION. © 2001 by Crossway Bibles, a division of Good News Publishers.

Scriptures marked KJV are from the KING JAMES VERSION (public domain).

Library of Congress Control Number: 2009943983

ISBN: 978-1-59555-305-8

Printed in the United States of America

10 11 12 13 HCI 1 2 3 4 5 6

For Marvin, Tim, Hamilton, and Topper.
The best mirror is an old friend.

CONTENTS

INTRODUCTION

According to legend, the man we know today as Saint Patrick was embarking on a ship bound for Ireland, when a leper accosted him. The outcast begged the holy man to let him come on the journey. Ever compassionate, Patrick was willing to let him come aboard. But the sailors and passengers would have none of it. Not only was the ship already full, but the leprous man "would be to them all at once an encumbrance and a horror."[1]

Patrick offered a solution that was both surprising and entirely characteristic of the saint of legend. He happened to have with him a stone altar, a gift from the pope himself, which he threw into the sea, and there it floated. He then instructed the leper to sit on the altar. When the ship sailed, the altar sailed beside it, all the way across the Irish Sea. When the vessel landed in Ireland, so did the leper and his makeshift boat. Patrick praised God, and the sailors' and passengers' stony hearts were transformed into hearts of compassion and charity.

This story is typical of the body of legend that grew up around Saint Patrick. The saint's compassion for the downtrodden is on full display. A former slave himself, Patrick was more attuned than most—even most saints—to matters of social justice. But even more uniquely Patrician is the sense of holy mirth that pervades the story. It's funny, that picture of a man riding a stone altar across the sea. There is more than simple humor happening here, however. This is divine comedy. In a comic reversal, the leper enjoyed a first-class berth—borne along on the mercy seat, you might say—while those who rejected him look on from the crowded deck.

The sheer volume of legends associated with Patrick—there are scores, even hundreds of them—is evidence of just how beloved he has been through the centuries. The most familiar images and tropes associated with Patrick tend to come from legends rather than the historical record. For example, Patrick did not run the snakes out of Ireland. Writing two hundred years *before* Patrick's time, the Greek geographer Solinus remarked that Ireland was free of snakes. There is no record of Patrick using the shamrock to teach the Irish about the Trinity. Neither did he have any dealings with leprechauns.

A remarkable number of the Patrick legends are comic, portraying the saint as a man you would enjoy being around. Consider, by contrast, Patrick's contemporary, Saint Augustine, with his towering intellect and moral and theological precision. You can't help respecting the man, but you wouldn't necessarily want him at your Christmas party.

Of the Patrick legends, nineteenth-century Irish poet Aubrey de Vere wrote, "Their predominant character is their brightness and gladsomeness."[2] In one story, Patrick was sitting with a friend named Vinnocus and discussing "things pertaining unto God," including "garments which by their works of mercy had been distributed among the poor." As they spoke of the cloaks they had given away, a cloak from heaven fell between them. An argument ensued between the holy men: Patrick insisted that the cloak was meant for Vinnocus, as a reward for his charitable spirit. Vinnocus insisted that it was Patrick who was being rewarded, for his willingness to give up all comfort for the sake of others. While they were "thus friendlily disputing," the cloak disappeared, and an angel arrived with two cloaks—one for each of them!—"that even in charity they might no longer contend."[3]

At times Patrick's comic reversals can seem cruel to modern sensibilities. For example, when one of Patrick's disciples laughs at a blind man who falls down as he runs to be healed, the saint heals the sightless man and blinds the scoffer.[4] And sometimes the humor is obvious but the point is obscure, as in the story of a thief who steals and eats a goat belonging to Patrick. When the thief denies his guilt, the goat begins bleating from inside his stomach.[5]

Some of the comic reversals in the Patrick legends are truly outlandish. In one tale, Patrick and his disciples were passing by a sepulchre "of wondrous length," so big that Patrick's followers refused to believe that any man could be buried there. Patrick, to prove that there was indeed a man in the tomb, prayed to bring him back to life. "Then stood one before them horrible in stature and in aspect." This terrifying giant broke down, weeping at the sight of Patrick, the man who had released him from the torments of hell. He then begged to join Patrick's retinue, but the saint refused him, fearful that no one could stand to look on such a terrifying figure as that "man of gigantic stature." He did, however, invite the giant to believe in the triune God and thus escape hell permanently. The giant believed, was baptized, died again, and was buried, this time to rest in peace.[6]

The monstrous, the horrible, the barbaric, folded into the love of a God who laughs. The terrible giant weeping for joy at the sight of the saint who released him from his torments. This is the divine comedy that shaped the career not just of the Patrick we know from legend, but the one we know from the historical record.

That historical record is admittedly brief. Everything we can reliably know of Patrick the man comes from two documents that, together, are fewer than twenty pages in length. Both were written by Patrick himself, late in his life. Though both contain autobiographical elements, neither is, properly speaking, an autobiography.

Patrick's *Confession* (also known as his *Declaration*) is a document of self-defense. After serving as a bishop in Ireland for an unspecified number of years, Patrick was charged with some wrongdoing or incompetence and was required to answer to his superiors back in Britain. He didn't spell out the charges against him (his original audience, after all, would have been well acquainted with the accusations), but they were most likely related to a perceived conflict between his mission to the unconverted Irish barbarians on the one hand, and his duties to the existing Christian community on the other. By definition, a bishop was responsible specifically for the *believers* under his authority. The local heathens didn't figure into the equation, except perhaps as enemies to the work of the Church. A "missionary bishop" would have been an utter novelty—and therefore very much in need of defending.

The second foundational document for the study of Patrick's life is his *Epistle to the Christian Subjects of the Tyrant Coroticus*. If Patrick was on the defensive in his *Confession*, in this second text he was very much on the offensive. The *Epistle*, known also as *A Letter to the Soldiers of Coroticus* and *St. Patrick's Epistle to Coroticus*, is a letter of excommunication for a nominally Christian warlord named Coroticus, who murdered, kidnapped, and enslaved a group of Patrick's newly baptized Irish converts (the anointing chrism, he wrote, "was still gleaming upon their foreheads"). The letter burns with a righteous and very personal anger that is the flip side of the tenderness he felt for his Irish flock.

Hard facts—in the form of specific dates and verifiable place names—are hard to come by in the *Confession* and the *Epistle*. But what Patrick's letters lack in details of his outward life, they more than make up for in their portrait of his inner life. He wrote in the *Confession*, "I want my brethren and kinsfolk to know my nature so that they may be able to perceive my soul's desire."[7] And he did reveal himself—his motivations, his doubts, his desires, his fears, his affections—to a remarkable degree in these two documents.

Patrick revealed, among other things, that he believed the gospel he preached. He believed that in Christ there is neither Jew nor Greek, male nor female, Roman nor barbarian. He believed that God can utterly transform a human heart. He believed that he could rely entirely on God's mercy, rather than being compelled to paper over his own sins. And he believed that even in the highly charged political atmosphere in which these letters were written and read, Christ was the defender of the weak—including Patrick himself.

Before moving forward, let me quickly outline the biographical facts that we do know. Patrick was a Roman Briton, born toward (or possibly after) the end of Roman rule in Britain—within a decade or two of AD 400. The son of a landowner who was also a local official and a deacon in the Roman Catholic Church, Patrick enjoyed a privileged childhood.

When he was about sixteen, Patrick's life of privilege and ease was interrupted by the arrival of Irish pirates, who kidnapped him (along with "thousands" of other Britons) and sold him into slavery. In the sheep pastures of his Irish owner, Patrick began for the first time to take ownership of the Christian faith in which he had been raised.

After six years of slavery, Patrick escaped, eventually making it back to Britain. He hadn't been home long, however, when a dream-vision convinced him that God was calling him back to Ireland to take the gospel to its people. Against his family's wishes, Patrick began taking the necessary steps to return to the land of his captivity. He resumed the education that had been interrupted by his enslavement, took holy orders, and eventually made it back to Ireland, where he became the first Christian missionary to take the gospel to barbarians beyond the borders of the Roman Empire.

Before Patrick, Christianity had never spread in any significant way outside the Roman Empire. Ireland was the first country ever to submit to the teachings of Christ without first submitting to the sword of Rome. It looked like a fool's errand, this mission to convert a people as wild and uncouth and violent as the Irish. And yet before he was finished, Patrick had laid the foundation for the near total Christianization of the island. In *How the Irish Saved Civilization*, Thomas Cahill shows that, thanks to the work of Saint Patrick, Ireland grew civilized even while civilization elsewhere in Western Europe collapsed: "As the Roman lands went from peace to chaos, the land of Ireland was rushing even more rapidly from chaos to peace."[8]

The achievements of the historical Patrick were no less miraculous than those of the legendary Patrick. Perhaps the most miraculous thing of all was that, even as he brought the gospel of Christ to bear on the Irish, Patrick left their Irishness intact. The Irish didn't have to become Roman in order to become Christian; that may seem obvious from where we sit, but it wasn't at all obvious in Patrick's time. His was a renewed vision of what it means to be a follower of Christ: just as the apostle Paul brought Christianity out from under the umbrella of Jewish culture, Patrick demonstrated that Christianity was bigger than the Roman Empire.

And that was no easy task.

THE BOY AT THE END
OF THE WORLD

For more than three centuries, the Romans ruled Britain. The occupation began in AD 43, when the emperor Claudius, with a herd of war elephants, crossed the Channel from Gaul. Impressed by the emperor and his elephants—though no doubt more impressed by the forty thousand Roman troops who had already won decisive victories in the southeast corner of the island—the petty kings of Britain surrendered en masse. Claudius, according to the inscription on an arch erected in his honor, "was the first to bring barbarian nations beyond the ocean under Roman sway."[1]

But by Patrick's time, Roman sway in Britain had itself begun to sway and to buckle beneath the constant pressure of surrounding tribes that refused to bow to the imperial yoke. Britain was the remotest extension of a badly overextended empire; by the latter half of the fourth century, Roman Britons—their Roman

towns and villas dotting a largely un-Romanized landscape—
would have been very conscious of the precariousness of their
situation.

The Romans dealt with insurgencies from local warlords
through much of their occupation of Britain, but AD 367
marked the beginning of troubles that would continue more or
less uninterrupted until the Roman army left Britain altogether.
The "Barbarian Conspiracy"—a well-coordinated offensive by
Picts, Scots, Saxons, and a tribe known as the Attacotti (who
hailed from Ireland)—threw the Roman army into disarray.
The barbarians pillaged and raped and murdered civilians
throughout the island. Not only was the army unable to protect
Roman citizens, but deserting soldiers also made matters worse
by joining the raiders in their devastation.

The army managed to regain control a year or two later,
sending the invaders back home. But the Barbarian Conspiracy
was a sign of things to come. Besides the outside threats it represented, it also intensified political power struggles that would
further destabilize the situation in Roman Britain.

Its distance from Rome made Britain a breeding ground
for usurpers, who used the island as a launching pad for their
personal ambitions. In 383, the usurper Magnus Maximus took
a large portion of the British garrison to Gaul in a bid to defeat
the unpopular emperor Gratian and solidify his own claim to the
throne. Maximus's usurpation was successful, but it left Roman
Britain more vulnerable than ever to attacks by neighboring
tribes, who marauded throughout the island until the Roman

general Stilicho drove them back across Hadrian's Wall—Roman Britain's border with the Picts and Scots—between 396 and 399. By 401, however, a legion from Hadrian's Wall was withdrawn from Britain to help deal with the Gothic tribes that were harassing Italy.

Indeed, the army's commitment to the defense of Britain rose and fell with the unstable situation on the Continent. On December 31, 406, tribes from eastern Europe—Vandals, Alans, and Sueves—crossed the frozen Rhine river and invaded Gaul, probably at Mainz, in modern-day Germany. This incursion, some four hundred miles distant from London, spelled the end for Roman Britain. Nervous about the westward sweep of the barbarians, British soldiers began electing their own emperors—three in a very short period of time. The first two didn't last more than a few months. The very soldiers who elected them put them to death when they didn't meet their expectations. The third, Constantine III, enjoyed more success than his predecessors because he did what the soldiers wanted him to do: in 407 he took most of the Roman army out of Britain to fight the barbarians in Gaul. They never came back.

In 410, the same year the Vandals sacked the city of Rome, the emperor Honorius "sent letters to the cities in Britain urging them to fend for themselves."[2] In so doing, he was only making official that which had been true on the ground for years: the empire lacked both the resources and the will to protect its most far-flung (and perhaps most troublesome) province. As Michael E. Jones has pointed out, it is noteworthy "that the emperor directed his reply to the cities—presumably because no duly constituted Roman authority any longer existed in Britain."[3] As one Roman historian put it, in 410 "Britain was forever removed from the Roman name."[4] The Anglo-Saxon invasions began about the time Honorius washed his hands of Britain; a new era had begun in earnest.

Such was the world in which Patrick grew up. He was a good Roman—a Latin-speaking son of Roman wealth and Roman privilege—in a land from which the Roman Empire was receding, never to return. Patrick's Roman bona fides were impeccable. His given name was the Latin *Patricius*, which means "highborn," and indeed he was. His father, Calpurnius (sometimes spelled Calpornius), was a Roman aristocrat—a landowner, town councilor, and deacon in the Roman Catholic Church.

After more than three hundred years of Roman rule, imperial influence persisted long after the army left the island. Britain's wealth was still concentrated in the hands of aristocratic Roman landowners, who, it appears, still dominated many town councils. Even more important, the Roman Catholic Church did much to preserve Roman culture and collective memory after Rome's governmental and military functions had left the island. The Church, in many ways, became a surrogate for the vanished empire.

What exactly would it mean to be a Roman aristocrat in a "post-Roman" world? Surely whatever privileges Patrick's family enjoyed as members of a ruling class would have been tempered by a deep sense of loss. They had inherited a rich cultural heritage, but now it was slipping away. On every side their wealth and their physical safety were threatened. They lived, in short, in a world that hadn't kept its promises.

~

We cannot know Patrick's exact dates. He didn't mention his birth year in either of his extant writings—there was no reason to—but he may have been born as early as the 380s, and he may have died as late as the 490s. The fact that he identified his father as a *decurion*, that is, a Roman official, suggests that he was born toward the earlier end of this range. If he had been born, say, in the 420s, well into the "sub-Roman" era of British history, it seems less likely that his childhood milieu would have been as fully Romanized as he described it. On the other hand, monks who claimed to have known him personally were still alive well into the sixth century, which would suggest that he lived toward the end of the fifth century. Though unlikely, it is possible that he lived 100 years, from the 390s into the 490s. One tradition has him living to 120, matching the life span of Moses! In any case, by the time he was born in Britain, the order and discipline associated with the Roman rule had clearly broken down.

In the opening lines of his *Confession*, Patrick reported that he was from a settlement called Bannaventa Burniae, but no one knows for sure where that was. There was a Bannaventa in what is now Northamptonshire, right in the heart of England, but the distance between there and the western coast would have been awfully far for Irish raiders to travel for booty. They would have been away from their boats a long time—and would have had to pass up many more convenient opportunities. Surely, if it was susceptible to Irish pirates, Patrick's Bannaventa Burniae was in the western reaches of Britain. A map of the villas that archaeologists have identified in Britain shows a much higher concentration of villas along the Bristol Channel than anywhere else along Britain's west coast. That area, where the southern coast of Wales meets England, seems as good a guess as any for the location of Patrick's boyhood home. If Britain was the edge of the civilized world, that western coast would have been the edge of the edge. Just across the narrow western sea was Ireland, a land the Romans never ruled. In the fourth and fifth centuries, the western coast of Britain was easy pickings for Irish raiders and slave traders.

~

The legends describe Patrick as an extremely pious child. In one, the infant Patrick miraculously provides the holy water for his own baptism! A blind and oddly underprepared priest, realizing that he doesn't have any water on hand, takes baby Patrick's hand and makes the sign of the cross over the ground. A spring of water bubbles forth, the baptism goes forward, and the blind priest receives sight when he washes his face with the water. What's more, the priest discovers that he is literate at his first sight of letters: he reads the words of the baptismal service.

Other stories have the boy Patrick using drops of water to start a fire and burning chunks of ice for firewood in order to show his nurse "how possible are all things to them who believe."[5] In another, when young Patrick discovers that a wolf has stolen a lamb that was under his watch, he prays and the wolf repents, bringing the lamb home the next day, unharmed (the story doesn't tell what the wolf and the lamb did together for a whole day).[6]

In many cases, the legends of Patrick illustrate and give color to the few facts we know of the saint. These stories of juvenile piety, however, are among the legends that flatly contradict what Patrick himself wrote. "I did not, indeed, know the true God," he said of his sixteen-year-old self.[7] Elsewhere he wrote, "I did not then believe in the living God, nor had I believed, since my infancy."[8] This from a man whose father was a deacon and his grandfather a priest.

Perhaps we shouldn't make too much of that. It is not unusual, after all, for a teenage boy to reject the faith of his parents. On the other hand, it is possible that young Patrick didn't know the true God because neither his father the deacon nor his grandfather the priest knew the true God. These relatives may have taken positions of church leadership not out of religious ardor, but for more worldly reasons.

As mentioned previously, Patrick's father, Calpurnius, in addition to being a deacon, was also a *decurion*—a member of the town council. It was a position of privilege, available only to the aristocracy. But the position had a significant downside.

Decurions were responsible for tax collection in the towns and villages where they served. Collections worked on a quota system: the government dictated to the decurion how much tax should be collected from his town. If there was any shortfall, the decurion was required to make up the difference out of his own pocket. The position, therefore, was a burdensome honor. Stressful and often expensive, it was also mandatory. A man appointed decurion couldn't get out of it; neither could his son, since, under Constantine the Great, the position became hereditary.

In the early- to mid-fourth century, however, Constantine created a loophole. Observing that many town councilors were also clergymen (both positions being drawn from the titled ranks), he exempted clergymen from decurion duty. Establishing Christianity as Rome's state religion was a big job; Constantine wanted the clergy to be able to focus on ecclesiastical matters. Not surprisingly, in the second half of the fourth century, there was a veritable epidemic of piety among decurions throughout the Empire. They joined the clergy in droves. To counteract this rush to ordination and to test the sincerity of the new town councilor-ordinands, a later reform required that any town councilor who joined the clergy would be required to sign over two-thirds of his estate to a relative.

Patrick didn't comment one way or another on his father's motives in becoming a deacon. Not that he would have: throughout his brief writings he was notably generous in his assessment of others. He didn't, in fact, mention his father's dual status—deacon and decurion—in the same document.

He identified Calpurnius as a deacon in his *Confession* and as a decurion in his *Epistle*, which is to say, he never drew attention to a circumstance that might cause a reader to be suspicious of his father's sincerity. Nevertheless, a reader familiar with the decurions' history of joining the clergy for worldly reasons can hardly help wondering what motivated Calpurnius.

Calpurnius's sincerity isn't really the point of this discussion, though. We could spin whole theories about Patrick's spiritual development and his vision of the Church and the world as a result of being raised by a religious charlatan, but there is no historical warrant for it. My real aim is to show how enmeshed worldly power and religious power had become in the fourth- and fifth-century Roman Empire.

There was a time in Church history when Christianity was a faith of outsiders. It began with fishermen and shepherds, slaves and women—people who could put little hope in their earthly prospects. The apostle Paul was speaking literally when he told the church at Corinth, "Not many of you were wise by human standards; not many were influential; not many were of noble birth. But God chose the foolish things of the world to shame the wise; God chose the weak things of the world to shame the strong. He chose the lowly things . . . and the despised things—and the things that are not—to nullify the things that are" (1 Corinthians 1:26–28).

In the first century or two of the faith, there was little earthly reason to claim the name of Christ. There were plenty of earthly reasons not to—not the least being the lions in the

Coliseum. Some children of Christian parents chose to embrace their parents' faith, and some chose not to. But it is hard to imagine such children making either choice casually.

By Patrick's time, however, it had been many long years since any Christian had been thrown to the lions. Christianity was the state religion, the status quo, in many cases a necessary step for social advancement. Especially in northern Europe, church leaders—bishops in particular—"tended to be drawn from the great territorial magnates who represented the old Roman administrative system."[9]

In Britain, especially, the class significance of Christianity was completely flip-flopped from the early centuries. There were bishoprics in Britain, yet it appears that the great majority of Christians (and not just the priests and bishops) came from the landowning class. Archaeologists have been able to find very little evidence of Christianity among the working classes, especially in the countryside. Chi-Rhos (symbols formed from the first two letters of the Greek word for Christ) have been found on luxury items, such as silver spoons and jewelry that were owned by the wealthy, but other than a private chapel in a Roman villa in Kent, archaeologists have had little luck identifying buildings that are unequivocally churches.[10] As E. A. Thompson has written, "Christianity (in so far as it existed) was an urban, and in the countryside an upper-class phenomenon, the religion of the landowners, in the last years of Roman Britain and in the following decades; and we should expect that those who were toiling in the fields were pagan almost to a man."[11]

If young Patrick paid little attention to the faith espoused by his father and grandfather, perhaps it was because Christianity was just what people of his station in life did. Perhaps he took it for granted the way he might have taken his Romanness for granted; he was born into it. Indeed, as far as Patrick's credentials as a Roman noble go, his father's association with the Roman Catholic Church may have meant more than his association with the Roman civil authority. As Thomas Cahill points out, the one office that survived in western Europe from the classical world through the medieval world and beyond was the Catholic bishop. In many districts, he wrote, the bishops were the "sole authority left, the last vestige of Roman law and order."[12]

Patrick's own journey toward the title of bishop would require that he first be cut off completely from the comparative stability represented by the Roman Catholic hierarchy. As a result, he would be a very different kind of bishop, one who would bring order to the chaos of Ireland, but not Roman order. That rupture in Patrick's life would come soon enough, in the form of Irish marauders crossing the western sea to snatch him away from the comfortable, privileged Roman life he enjoyed. Before those marauders swoop down, though, let us consider one last moment from that pre-Irish period of Patrick's life.

In his *Confession*, Patrick wrote of some sin that, he said, "I had perpetrated on a day, nay, rather in one hour—in my boyhood because I was not yet . . . [self-controlled]. God knows—I do not—whether I was then fifteen years old at the time."[13]

He confessed this sin to a friend before he was ordained as a deacon. Years later, this same friend made an issue of Patrick's boyhood crime when he was up for bishop.

Saint Augustine, Patrick's contemporary, famously admitted to a boyhood sin in his own *Confessions*, that of fruit-stealing (though he also confessed to other, graver sins from later in adolescence and manhood). Clearly, the sin to which Patrick referred was something more serious than stealing fruit. He was bothered enough by it to confess it to a friend some fifteen years later (assuming he was fifteen when he committed the sin and thirty when he was made a deacon, a typical minimum age for a deacon of the era). More significant, the friend to whom Patrick confessed remembered the sin some twenty years later (fifty being a typical minimum age for a bishop), and it seemed relevant to the men who were deciding whether or not to make him a bishop.

What sin, committed in a single hour by a fifteen-year-old boy, would be so serious that it would still be considered significant when he was fifty? Sexual indiscretion comes to mind; a teenager doesn't even need an hour to head down that path. But surely even the most censorious council of bishops couldn't get too wound up about such a thing thirty-five years later.

It seems the only sin Patrick could be talking about is homicide. Perhaps in a moment of rage or carelessness, the young Patrick impulsively killed one of the slaves who worked the family's lands. He could get away with it: after all, he was the son of the lord of the manor. But as time went on—and he found himself in the position of slave, his heart changed by the love of God—the gravity of his crime dawned on him.

We will return to Patrick's childhood sin—or, more to the point, to his enemies' use of it—in a later chapter. For now, the clouds are gathering on the western horizon, across the western sea.

2

"IN THE LAND OF
MY CAPTIVITY"

Britain may have seemed uncivilized compared, say, to the parts of the Roman Empire that ringed the Mediterranean, but it was downright urbane compared to Ireland. Pomponius Mela, writing in AD 44, said of the Irish, "The inhabitants of this island are unrefined, ignorant of all the virtues more than any other people, and totally lacking all sense of duty."[1] Ever suspicious of the peoples who lived beyond the reach of their civilizing influence, the Greeks and Romans told (and believed) many tall tales about the barbarians. Some of the tallest they reserved for the Irish, whom they called *Scoti* or *Atticoti*.

In the classical imagination, Irish barbarism rose to mythic levels. In AD 19, the Greek geographer Strabo wrote of Ireland, "The people living there are more savage than the Britons, being cannibals as well as gluttons. Further, they consider it honorable to eat their dead fathers and to openly have intercourse, not only with unrelated women, but with their mothers and sisters as well."[2] Though he admitted that he had no reliable witnesses to confirm these calumnies against the Irish, he reasoned that since other barbarians were "known" to practice cannibalism, he could be confident in his characterization of the Irish.

For both Strabo and Pomponius Mela, Ireland seemed impossibly remote, the edge not only of the inhabited world, but also of the *habitable* world. Earlier geographers (including Strabo) believed Ireland to be north of Britain rather than west, and therefore considerably more frigid. Its "completely wild people live a wretched existence on account of the cold," wrote Strabo.[3] One gets the sense that no civilized or even sane person would *try* to live in such a place as Ireland.

Strabo and Pomponius Mela were writing three or four hundred years before Patrick, at a time when even Britain seemed to be beyond the end of the world. But Roman attitudes toward the Irish hadn't necessarily changed much by Patrick's time. Consider what Saint Jerome had to say in the early fifth century:

> Why should I speak of other nations when I myself as a young man in Gaul saw the Atticoti [or Scoti], a British people, feeding on human flesh? Moreover, when they come across herds of pigs and cattle in the forests, they frequently cut off the buttocks of the shepherds and their wives, and their nipples, regarding these alone as delicacies. The nation of the *Scoti* do not have individual wives, but, as if they had read Plato's

Republic or followed the example of Cato, no wife belongs to a particular man, but as each desires, they indulge themselves like beasts.[4]

As Philip Freeman points out, Jerome was in Gaul in 367, the year of the Barbarian Conspiracy in Britain. It is possible that he saw Irish raiders who had crossed the Channel to extend their pillage into Gaul. But did he actually encounter Irishmen feeding on human flesh? It seems more likely, as Freeman says, that Jerome encountered "rough-and-ready foreign soldiers having fun with a gullible Roman youth over a meal of mutton stew."[5]

Let us assume that Jerome had it wrong. Perhaps he was fusing what he had seen (Irish invaders in Gaul) with what he had heard about them (that they practiced an especially grisly form of cannibalism). If so, how was it possible for even a gullible young Roman to believe such things? What made it possible for that same person to believe such things in middle age and expect his reader to believe them? For Strabo, the Irish might as well have been space aliens. He was never going to see one, or even see anyone who *had* seen one. He could believe anything about the Irish. Not so for Jerome. In his and Patrick's era, there was some limited trade between Ireland and Rome—and some limited war too. Jerome had seen Irishmen with his own eyes. And from what he had observed, he could well imagine them eating the buttocks and nipples off of shepherds and their wives.

The Irish were a Celtic people who migrated to the island from the Continent (or perhaps from Britain) no later than the fourth century BC. The Celts dominated large swaths of Europe during the Iron Age, from Asia Minor to the Iberian Peninsula to Gaul (modern-day France) and Britain. The Greeks and Romans who first encountered the Celts were struck by their warlike spirit and a bravery that verged on foolhardiness. Throughout the classical sources, the Celts (or Gauls, as they were often called) are portrayed as immoderate, even extravagant in all things—great feasters and boasters, brawlers and headhunters. This extravagance was their chief weakness as well as their chief strength.

The Greek Diodorus, writing in the first century BC, offers a colorful description of the Celts' battle practices:

> Some of them are so unafraid of death that they come into the battle naked except for a loincloth . . . When the warriors face each other on the field of battle, one will often go in front of his companions and challenge the best of the other side to single combat while showing off his weapons and trying to fill his opponents with fear. If someone accepts his challenge, he will begin boasting about the courage of his ancestors and describing his own brave deeds while mocking and belittling his challenger, all in an attempt to destroy his opponent's courage with words.[6]

Diodorus goes on to say that the Celts cut off their enemies' heads and decorated their houses with them, proudly showing them to visitors.

According to Posidonius, a Greek from the first century BC, Celtic feasts could be quite dangerous. The bravest man in the room claimed the choice thigh portion of the meat. If any man challenged him over it, the two men would fight to the death. Diodorus describes an immoderate love of wine among the Celts, though, to be fair to the Celts, Greeks tended to level the same charge at all barbarian people groups: "The Gauls are crazy for wine and consume, unwatered, amazing amounts imported by merchants. Their unrestrained consumption often leads them to fall into a drunken stupor or fall into morose depression."[7]

For the Greeks and Romans, the immoderate Celts served as a foil for the moderation and discipline they valued in their own civilizations—and they tended to write to that script when they wrote about the Celts. For that reason, we should take all classical descriptions of Celts with a grain of salt. Perhaps it would be more helpful to speak of these tribal people as whole-hearted, rather than extravagant or immoderate.

Caesar's campaigns in Gaul in 58–51 BC marked the end of the Celtic ascendancy in northern Europe. As the centuries progressed, the Celts succumbed to the civilizing influence of their Roman conquerors. Throughout the Continent, the wild Celts became good Romans (though less so in Britain). And they made their own contributions to the empire. They were valued as soldiers, as artisans, and as orators.

The Irish, however, on their remote, green island, were a sort of time capsule of Iron Age Celtic culture. In the absence of significant external forces, their tribal, agricultural, warlike society stayed very much the same for a very long time.

Ireland had no central government. Instead, it had a hundred or more petty kings, each ruling a *tuatha*, or tribe. This tuatha might be as small as a few hundred people, or it might include thousands, but it was very much a local unit. An individual's rights were protected within his or her tuatha; outside the tuatha, however, there were no guarantees. Only three classes of people were guaranteed safe passage from tuatha to tuatha: kings, priests, and poets. A preliterate society, the Irish particularly valued poets for their ability to preserve (and create) their oral tradition.

Ireland's landscape was dominated by forest and bogs, which meant that settlements would have been spread apart and inaccessible to one another, contributing to an insularity and clannishness comparable to that of the Scottish Highlands or, to a lesser degree, the hills and hollows of Appalachia. Such settlements in fifth-century Ireland would have looked more like forest clearings than anything we might identify as towns or villages.[8]

The Irish were farmers and herders. They measured their wealth in cattle. Not surprisingly, the practice of cattle raiding was almost as widespread as that of cattle raising, joining as it does the Irish passions for fighting and for cattle. Cattle raiding was so deeply ingrained in the culture of the Irish, in fact, that one of the great epics of the Irish literary tradition, *Táin Bó Cúailnge* (or, *The Cattle Raid of Cooley*), is the story of a cattle raid pursued on a grand scale, a whole army staging an invasion to steal a prize bull from a neighboring kingdom.

The druids, the priests of Ireland's pre-Christian tradition, figure hugely in the Patrick legends, but we don't know a great deal about them. It seems that an important role of the druid was to serve as a repository of the culture's lore and history. According to Caesar, they were also arbiters of justice. Their training, wrote Pomponius Mela, lasted up to twenty years and consisted of memorizing huge amounts of secret lore. They wrote none of their learning down, but passed it orally from druid to druid.[9] According to Pliny the Elder, the word *druid* means "oak-knower," but this was a false etymology. Still, it does seem likely that the religion of the druids was animistic and included some communication with and through the phenomena of the natural world. Classical writers, including Caesar, described human sacrifice as being part of the druids' priestly duties. The classical writers aren't always reliable on the subject of Celtic culture, but there is ample archaeological evidence of human sacrifice in the pre-Christian rituals of the British Isles.[10]

Irish religion, like Irish government, was a local affair. Each locality had its own gods and goddesses. Each earthly king was considered the mate of the local goddess. Goddesses, for the most part, were responsible for the natural world. For example, there would be a goddess for a particular stream, for an oak tree, for fertility. Gods, on the other hand, were connected with human arts and institutions—war, for example, individual crafts, or feasting. There was no "Irish" pantheon per se, for the deities of one tribe wouldn't be the deities of the next.

There was a strong otherworldly element to Irish religion. This otherworld was known as the *sídhe* (its inhabitants were also known as the sídhe), and is best thought of not as the place of the afterlife (though it is that too), but as a parallel, alternate reality. Most of the Irish myths hinge on gods and goddesses of the sídhe—partially humanized—coming to this world, and/or people from this world going to the sídhe.

A myth known as "The Labor Pains of the Ulaid" is typical: A beautiful woman turns up at the house of a widower named Cruinniuc and begins performing the duties of a wife as if she had always been there. Her very presence brings prosperity to the man and his sons. When fair time comes around, Cruinniuc's mysterious wife is pregnant and close to giving birth. She warns Cruinniuc not to say anything foolish at the fair—a clear indication that we can expect Cruinniuc to say something foolish.

At the chariot races, the king's horses beat all comers. The host marvels, "Nothing is as fast as those horses are." In spite of his wife's warning, Cruinniuc can't keep his mouth shut. He blurts out, "My wife is that fast." The king and the fairgoers are understandably intrigued. They insist on seeing a race between Cruinniuc's wife and the king's horses. Cruinniuc's wife tries to beg off on the grounds that she is pregnant, but she is forced to run: the king will kill her husband if she doesn't. The woman does outrun the horses, but the strain of the running sends her into labor. As she struggles to give birth right there on the racecourse, she declares that any man who hears her screams will suffer the pains of labor for nine days. The story explains why the Ulaid—the tribe that forced the woman to run—were as weak as a laboring woman for nine generations.[11]

The mysterious woman, of course, is of the sídhe. She is a personified horse goddess named Macha. These deities come and they go. They shift shapes and reshape the mortal world. They draw mortals into the sídhe, then deposit them back in their own world with no notice—and not always at the original point of departure! But they do not exert any consistent moral authority. In Macha's story, her judgment against the Ulaid is an answer to their lack of compassion for a pregnant woman, but in just as many cases, the Irish deities' actions seem completely arbitrary. Any Irish looking for moral guidance would have needed to look elsewhere besides their myths.

≈

It was by conquering that the Roman army brought a new social order to the Celts of the Continent and Britain. It was by retreating that they brought a new social order to the Celts of Ireland. The army's departure from Britain—and the power vacuum it created—was the outside impetus that finally brought significant change to Ireland's centuries-old, Iron Age society. Liam de Paor speaks of a dawning "heroic age" in fourth- and fifth-century Ireland. Easy loot from a weakened Britain suddenly transformed Irish social dynamics that had changed very little in eight hundred years and more. De Paor wrote:

> This is what constitutes an "heroic age": that a people sub-sisting stably on pasture and tillage, with a simple system of customary law and an already established social hierarchy, is provided with an opportunity to prey on a rich, highly orga-nized and prestigious civilization. And in the heroic age of the fourth and fifth centuries in Ireland, chieftains who could organize well-equipped raiding bands, arrange shipping, and conduct the necessary negotiations with other likeminded leaders (whether Irish or Pictish), were able to enrich them-selves with loot and slaves.[12]

Raids and battles had always been a fact of Irish life, but until now they had only shifted wealth and relative power from one part of the island to another. They had never tilted the social equilibrium the way the sudden influx of wealth from Roman Britain did. A new class of warrior kings was emerging—kings capable of consolidating power in a way that the local, patriar-chal kings never had.

Across the Irish Sea, these seismic shifts would have the most direct and personal effect imaginable on a teen named Patrick.

≈

"I was taken into captivity in Ireland with many thousands of people, according to our deserts," wrote Patrick in his *Confession*, "for quite drawn away from God, we did not keep his precepts, nor were we obedient to our priests who used to remind us of our salvation."[13] Where the historian sees impersonal political, military, and social forces, Patrick saw the hand of God. The Irish robbers who swept through his villa and carried Patrick and others into slavery were agents of divine justice whether they knew it or not.

"And the Lord brought down on us the fury of his being," Patrick continued, "and scattered us among many nations, even to the ends of the earth."[14] This is the language of Old Testament prophecy; perhaps the most important echo is from Jeremiah 9:16, in which God warns a complacent Judah of their coming exile: "I will scatter them among nations that neither they nor their fathers have known." The Britons, like the Israelites, had had every opportunity to respond to the overtures of a loving God. But like the Israelites, they had remained cold—and had thus been scattered among the heathens. Patrick viewed his personal calamity as part of a larger, national judgment. When he spoke of being taken with "many thousands of people," he didn't mean one particular raid. He was talking about years of raids up and down Britain's western coast.

When Patrick wrote that his fellow Britons were scattered to "the ends of the earth," he was speaking quite literally. So far as he knew, Ireland was indeed the end of the earth. There was nothing beyond but ocean. But even in that little phrase there is hope, for it conjures up God's promise to the Israelites after their punishment was done: "I will . . . make you a light for the Gentiles, that you may bring my salvation to the ends of the earth" (Isaiah 49:6). Writing fifty years or more after that dreadful day, Patrick could see that his capture by Irish pirates was the first step in his lifework of bringing salvation to the ends of the earth.

It may be worth noting that this passage from Isaiah is the very text the apostle Paul quoted when the Jews challenged him for preaching the gospel to the Gentiles (Acts 13:47). Patrick found himself in a similar situation as he wrote his *Confession*. Called out by a church hierarchy who believed the gospel was only for the civilized, he had to defend himself for preaching it to barbarians.

≈

As is typical of Patrick's writing, he had more to say about the internal or spiritual facts of his slavery than he did about the external, physical facts. He never named his master or gave any other details about him (later tradition identifies him as a petty king named Miliucc). Neither did he say where in Ireland he spent his years of servitude. It was probably somewhere near Ireland's west coast; when he escaped, he had to travel two hundred Roman miles to catch a ship headed toward Britain— which, presumably, would be leaving from Ireland's east coast. To be that many miles from an eastern port, he would have to be pretty far west. Later in life, when he received the call to return to Ireland, he heard "the voice of those very people who [lived] near the wood of Foclut, which is near the Western Sea," and they begged him, "Come and walk among us."[15] Scholars associate the wood of Foclut (or Voclut) with the Wood of Fochoill, in County Mayo, in the northwest portion of Ireland.

Patrick could hardly have experienced a more complete reversal of fortune. The aristocratic Roman—likely from a family that had slaves of its own—was out of the comfort of the villa and slaving in a sheep pasture in a barbarian country. The physical conditions were harsh: he wrote of a work environment marked by snow, ice, and rain.

Patrick's outward reversal resulted in an inward reversal that was no less dramatic. There in the meadow, away from home and stripped of everything—including the organized religion of his forefathers—Patrick turned at last to the God he had heard about all his life. Indeed, where else could he turn?

> There the Lord opened my mind to an awareness of my unbelief, in order that, [perhaps], I might remember my transgressions and turn with all my heart to the Lord my God, who had regard for my insignificance and pitied my youth and ignorance. And he watched over me before I knew him, and before I learned sense or even distinguished between good and evil, and he protected me, and consoled me as a father would his son.[16]

There, watching over his master's sheep, Patrick realized that the Good Shepherd had been watching over him all along. The God who had poured down his "fury" was now binding up young Patrick's wounds, comforting the wayward boy as a father comforts his son.

Growing up in church, Patrick had paid little or no attention to the things of God. But isolated in a field full of sheep, a holy zeal began to burn in Patrick that would eventually transform all of Irish culture. "More and more did the love of God, and my fear of him and faith increase," Patrick wrote, "and my spirit was moved so that in a day [I would say as many as] a hundred prayers, and in the night a like number."[17]

It was this fervent inner life that got Patrick through the physical hardships of his everyday life. More than tolerating his difficult duties, he rejoiced through them, springing to life in the morning. "I would wake up before daylight to pray, in the snow, in icy coldness, in rain, and I used to feel neither ill nor any slothfulness, because . . . the Spirit was burning in me."[18]

Eugene Peterson speaks of the "God-dominated imagination" that developed in David as he spent his days and nights watching sheep on the Judean hillsides.[19] It appears that something similar happened in Patrick. In the lush, green hills of western Ireland, in the towering clouds that rolled across the big sky, even in the most inclement of weather, Patrick sensed the presence of a Creator who hadn't seemed very real or relevant or necessary in his earlier life of ease. For all its disadvantages, the shepherd's life leaves plenty of time to think and pray, and Patrick used his time to great advantage. Far from wallowing in self-pity, Patrick celebrated his enslavement, the very shock he needed to bring him to his senses.

Throughout his *Confession*, Patrick's language is shot through with the confidence that, whatever his circumstances, God was doing good things in his life. He viewed his kidnapping and slavery as God's direct work; this work, however, was not merely punitive but remedial, not evidence that God had forsaken him, but that God wished to draw Patrick to himself. So rather than growing bitter, Patrick allowed God's chastisement to do its work in him. His enslavement, he believed, was a hard mercy, but a mercy nonetheless.

From the very beginning of the *Confession*, we get a glimpse of Patrick's indomitable joy. His tone echoed that of Paul, who wrote from prison,

> I have learned to be content whatever [my] circumstances. I know what it is to be in need, and I know what it is to have plenty. I have learned the secret of being content in any and every situation, whether well fed or hungry, whether living in plenty or in want. I can do everything through him who gives me strength (Philippians 4:11–13).

Those six years, from age sixteen to twenty-two, laid an unassailably strong foundation for Patrick's future ministry.

3

A LONG JOURNEY HOME

After six years of slavery, Patrick had the first of the many dream-visions that he describes in the *Confession*. In his sleep, he heard a voice saying, "You do well to fast: soon you will depart for your home country." Not long afterward, he heard another voice: "Behold, your ship is ready." So he left: "I turned about and fled from the man with whom I had been for six years."[1]

It seems clear from Patrick's language that he ran away. He wasn't released by his master; neither did he buy his freedom. To Patrick's straightforward description of his escape, however, the later legends add a few details that would seem to absolve him of the "crime" of running away from the man who had paid good money for him. It seems that the hagiographers (people who write about the lives of saints) were not comfortable with the possibility that Patrick had not followed Paul's injunction to slaves to obey their earthly masters (Ephesians 6:5; Colossians 3:22).

According to a story from Jocelin's *Life and Acts of St. Patrick*, the angel who announced that Patrick would soon go home also showed him a hole in the ground in which he found "no small weight of gold"[2] with which to buy back his freedom. Having paid off Milcho, his "hard and cruel master,"[3] Patrick went his merry way. But Milcho changed his mind. Like the Pharaoh who pursued the Israelites after letting them go, he took off after the valuable slave he had released, which, presumably, explains why Patrick claims to have "fled" a master from whom he had not escaped. Milcho, by the way, received an additional insult, according to the story: when he gave up the chase and went home, the gold had disappeared![4]

Patrick felt no need to apologize for his flight or to justify it. He didn't even say anything about his master being a cruel man. Patrick simply believed God's authority to be higher than his master's authority. He understood his slavery to be a sort of apprenticeship in the humility that would mark the rest of his life and ministry. The apprenticeship over, he moved on.

The ship that awaited Patrick was two hundred miles away. It is hard to imagine how an escaped slave could have made it that far across a landscape like that of fifth-century Ireland. According to Liam de Paor, "Numerous undrained lakes and river valleys and lowlands created many watery wildernesses in which the traveling stranger would be almost literally at sea."[5] The impossible topography (and the fact that there were no roads) would have been only the beginning of Patrick's problems. The dangers from the people he met would have been terrifying, with new dangers each time he entered a different settlement. An Irishman would have been in grave danger traveling cross-country out of his *tuatha*—how much more for a slave and a foreigner? Every word Patrick spoke would have revealed his foreignness—and vulnerability. Like escaped slaves throughout history, he likely traveled at night. But how did he navigate strange bogs, forests, and rivers in the dark? And with no money, how could he feed himself on such a long journey?

Not surprisingly, Patrick attributed his success and safety to the guiding hand of God. "[He] directed my route to advantage," he wrote, adding that he was afraid of nothing in his travels[6]—perhaps the greatest miracle of the whole journey.

Patrick's tale gets stranger when he makes it to the ship. In some ways, the next section of his account offers more narrative detail than he usually gave. But the details don't add up to a coherent story. Scholars have wrestled with these problems for many years, and they won't get solved here. But we will make sense of them the best we can.

When Patrick finally arrived at the sea, the ship he sought was getting ready to sail. He approached the steersman, announcing that he "had the wherewithal" to sail with him.[7] To what might this "wherewithal" refer? As a slave, surely he couldn't have possessed enough coin to pay for his passage. However, a few lines down he mentioned a hut where he had been staying, so it is possible that he had found a job nearby and had made a little money. Most likely, though, he simply meant that he would be able to work for his passage. But after traveling two hundred miles by foot and with no money, he couldn't have cut a very impressive figure.

Indeed, the captain appears to have been utterly unimpressed with Patrick. He refused Patrick's request and was none too polite about it. Patrick wrote that "the steersman was displeased and replied in anger, sharply."[8]

Surely dejected at being refused after so long a trip—not to mention confused about God's purposes—Patrick headed back to the hut where he had stayed, praying as he walked. Before his prayer was finished, a sailor came running after him, calling him back to the ship. The captain had changed his mind.

Besides an answer to prayer, what might have changed the captain's mind so quickly? Perhaps he recognized a business opportunity: he could sell this escaped slave back into slavery once they crossed the sea.

Welcoming Patrick on board, the sailors told him, "Because we are admitting you out of good faith, make friendship with us in any way you wish."[9] It seems they were inviting him to participate in a strange and obscure pagan custom, because in his next sentence Patrick remarked that he "refused to suck [their] breasts." The reader gets the feeling that, by getting mixed up with these sailors, Patrick had entered into a bizarre and alien world. Author Philip Freeman has identified stories in which breast sucking—including breast sucking between adult males—is a sign of bonding and adoption. He speaks in particular of a medieval tale in which a dwarf sucks at the breast of an Irish king to signify submission and friendship.[10] Yet even if breast sucking were a token of friendship, it seems it would also signify dependence, not an equal friendship. In any case, Patrick refused the offer because of the "fear of God."[11] He had no desire to join his shipmates in their heathen practices.

After a three-day journey, the ship made landfall, though whether in Britain or in Gaul remains under scholarly debate. Wherever they landed, according to Patrick, they traveled for twenty-eight days "through uninhabited country."[12] This is one of the biggest mysteries in Patrick's story. Where—in Britain or in Gaul—would there have been an uninhabited region so vast that you could wander in it for nearly a month? It is tempting to say that Patrick was speaking allegorically here—that the twenty-eight days of wandering represent some spiritual or biblical truth. But no biblical parallel offers itself.

The huge wasteland of which Patrick wrote gives us the biggest reason to doubt that he was in Britain, because it is small enough that the crew could hardly wander for twenty-eight days without going in circles. Second, compared to Ireland or much of Gaul, Britain was densely populated. It is hard to imagine any large area that could be described as "uninhabited."

In truth, there would have been no swath of "uninhabited country" in western Europe that would have taken four full weeks to cross, though it seems more likely in Gaul than in Britain. Perhaps the crew were shipwrecked and landed in an

unknown region of Gaul. If this is the case, however, it is surprising that Patrick didn't mention it. To add a shipwreck to his
résumé would have made for yet another impressive parallel to
the apostle Paul's career.

One possibility worth considering is that they wandered in
an area that was deserted because of war and invasion. Could this
have been the aftermath of the same Vandal invasion of 406–7
that led to the Roman army's final departure from Britain? It's
a tantalizing possibility, but a highly speculative one, and there
is no reason to believe those invasions (or any other) left huge
areas completely deserted.

In short, this is a frustrating portion of the *Confession*: it's
one of the few places where Patrick offered what appear to be
specific biographical details, and yet it is very hard to take those
details literally. He was, though, probably writing forty to fifty
years after the events he was describing; perhaps a few days of
being lost and hungry got exaggerated in his mind, growing to
twenty-eight days.

E. A. Thompson has raised the possibility that Patrick was
being intentionally deceptive in this section, to conceal the fact
that the sailors with whom he was traveling were actually pirates
who had crossed the sea for pillage. His purpose in writing the
Confession, after all, was to defend his character and his career.
It wouldn't do to have people finding out that he had ever con-
sorted with pirates. But Thompson freely admits that the idea
is wildly speculative—more thought experiment, really, than
actual theory, and one, we should add, that does some violence

to what little we can confidently know of Patrick.[13] And since this is mere speculation, let us be content (or not) to say that Patrick and his shipmates found themselves lost and starving in a remote area of either Britain or Gaul.

When the food was gone, the captain—still surly, still suspicious of the Roman Christian in their midst—began to mock Patrick: "Why is it, Christian? You say your God is great and all-powerful; then why can you not pray for us? For we may perish of hunger; it is unlikely indeed that we shall ever see another human being."[14]

The scene is vaguely reminiscent of Jonah: the man of God was in the midst of pagan sailors at the brink of disaster. And like Jonah, Patrick took responsibility for fixing the situation. He was glad for the chance to pray, to demonstrate the power of his God, and perhaps to bring some of these Irish sailors to a saving knowledge of Christ. He wrote, "[But] I said to them confidently, 'Be converted by faith with all your heart to my Lord God, because nothing is impossible for him, so that today he will send food for you on your road, until you be sated, because everywhere he abounds.'"[15]

In answer to Patrick's prayer, a herd of pigs appeared before them on the road. The sailors' hunger turned to feasting. For two days they sated themselves on pork, and afterward "gave the utmost thanks to God." They even came to honor Patrick.[16]

In addition to pork, the sailors found wild honey. They offered some to Patrick, saying that it was a "sacrifice." This was possibly an attempt on their part to worship Patrick, the man who, they believe, had rescued them from starvation. Patrick had just remarked, after all, that he had become "esteemed in their eyes." The usual interpretation, though, is that the soldiers had sacrificed the honey (or some portion of it) to their pagan gods. Either way, Patrick, still diligent to avoid even the appearance of paganism, refused to have any.[17]

One common perception of Patrick is that, as the father of Celtic Christianity, he was somehow syncretistic or not quite orthodox in his faith. The idea persists that he reached the polytheistic Irish by mixing pagan and Christian ideas and practices. In the *Confession*, however, Patrick diligently demonstrated his Roman Catholic credentials. He conspicuously refused heathen practices, though, notably, he was neither combative nor scolding toward his pagan shipmates.

The appearance of the pigs was the young holy man's greatest—certainly his most spectacular—triumph to date. It caused men who worshipped many gods to both give thanks to the one true God and to revere his servant Patrick. This achievement, however, was immediately followed by one of those dark nights of the soul that so often come after great triumphs: "The very same night while I was sleeping Satan attacked me violently, as I will remember as long as I shall be in this body; and there fell on top of me as it were, a huge rock, and not one of my members had any force."[18]

The prophet Elijah had a similar experience. Immediately after his greatest triumph—his defeat of the four hundred prophets of Baal—he lost heart completely. When Queen

Jezebel threatened to kill him, he ran away in terror, completely forgetting the awe-inspiring power that God had put at his disposal just a little while earlier. (1 Kings 18:25–39; 19:1–4.)

Patrick experienced this same spiritual letdown in the form of Satan, heavy as a boulder, pinning and immobilizing him on the ground. It was clearly a terrifying experience: Patrick said that for the rest of his life he would remember that utter helplessness at the hands of the enemy of his soul. In the absence of his own strength, Patrick called out for the strength of another— Elijah, as it turned out: "But from whence did it come to me, ignorant in the spirit, to call upon 'Helias' [Elijah]? And meanwhile I saw the sun rising in the sky, and while I was crying 'Helias, Helias' with all my might, lo, the brilliance of that sun fell on me and immediately shook me free of all the weight."[19]

There is a complicated bit of wordplay here. Patrick called on Elijah by his Latin name, Helias. Having summoned Helias, though, what he got was *helios*, the sun, rising and bringing relief from his tortured dream. At first blush this looks like a mishmash of Christianity and pagan sun worship, but Patrick made it clear, before the sentence even ended, that it was Christ who was at work, first and last: "I believe that I was aided by Christ my Lord."

Near the end of the *Confession*, Patrick further addressed the connection between the sun and the Son of God: "For the sun we see rises each day for us at [Christ's] command, but it will never reign, neither will its splendour last; but all people who worship it will come wretchedly to punishment. We, on the other hand, shall not die, who believe in and worship the true sun, Christ, who will never die; no more shall he die who has done Christ's will."[20] The sun is a created good, he was saying, a blessing, but not worthy of our worship. The true sun is Christ himself.

The sun that rose on Patrick and relieved him that morning is the same sun of righteousness of which the prophet Malachi wrote as he relayed the words of God to a wayward nation: "For you who revere my name, the sun of righteousness will rise with healing in its wings . . . See, I will send you the prophet Elijah before that great and dreadful day of the LORD comes" (Malachi 4:2, 5). There's Elijah again.

There is yet another pun that seems to be at work in this passage. Christ on the cross, in his moment of greatest distress, cried out "*Eloi, Eloi, lama sabachthani?*"—that is, "My God, my God, why have you forsaken me?" In Patrick's anguished cry "*Helias, Helias,*" we hear an echo of Jesus' "*Eloi, Eloi.*" Those who heard Jesus' cry thought he was calling on Elijah (Elias). The "intentional confusion" of *Helias* and *helios* seems to parallel the confusion of Eloi and Elias at Calvary.

If there are multilingual puns and complex biblical references here, Patrick made a point of saying that he was unaware of them at the time. His education—religious and otherwise—had gotten interrupted, and he indicated that what religious training he did receive, he gave little attention. So his question, "From whence did it come to me, ignorant in the spirit, to call upon 'Helias'?" was a fair one.

He answered his own question: "I believe that I was aided by Christ my Lord, and that his Spirit then was crying out for me . . . just as it says in the Gospel: 'In that hour,' the Lord declares, 'it is not you who speaks but the Spirit of your Father speaking in you.'"[21] Christ prayed on Patrick's behalf; Christ answered the prayer; Christ *was* the answer to the prayer. Christ is all in all.

The poem/prayer known as "Saint Patrick's Breastplate" was probably not written by Saint Patrick. But one section gives voice to Patrick's Christ-filled vision:

> Christ with me, Christ before me, Christ behind me,
>   Christ in me!
> Christ below me, Christ above me.
> Christ at my right, Christ at my left!
> Christ in breadth, Christ in length, Christ in height!"[22]

In the face of Satan's oppression, the answer for Patrick was the full presence of Christ, who didn't wait for Patrick to know how to call out for him. This is an important point in Patrick's theology, the idea that Christ was at work in him and through him quite independent of his ability or wisdom or eloquence. It appears again and again in his writing.

≈

Immediately after the *Helias/helios* episode, Patrick reported an incident that seems entirely out of place: "And a second time, after many years, I was taken captive. On the first night I accordingly remained with my captors, but I heard a divine prophecy, saying to me: 'You shall be with them for two months.' So it happened. On the sixtieth night the Lord delivered me from their hands."[23]

When did this second, sixty-day captivity happen? Many years after what? If he meant many years after his escape from Ireland, why did he mention it here? If he meant many years (i.e., six) after his first capture, that seems a strange qualifier. Is six years really "many" years? That seems a better of two bad choices. Assuming that six years from his first capture was *many* years to him, and this second captivity occurred between the time the herd of swine turned up on the road and when he made it home, then it seems likely that Patrick wasn't captured so much as sold. It's not hard to imagine his shipmates turning on him and selling him back into slavery. Or he, perhaps along with some of his shipmates, might have been caught by passing slavers.

The later legends include a funny story about this captivity. According to the story, after Patrick and the sailors went their separate ways, Patrick fell into the hands of strangers, who traded him to a man for a kettle. But when they went to heat water in the kettle, the water got colder instead of hotter. The more wood they put on the fire, the colder the water got, until they ended up with a kettle of ice over a roaring fire. Thinking the kettle had been enchanted, they took it back to Patrick's new master. When he put the kettle over the fire, the water got hot with no problem. By that everyone knew that Patrick had been wronged, and they released him to go home to his family.[24]

And so shall we.

4

"WALK AGAIN AMONG US"

After a few years," Patrick wrote matter-of-factly, "I was again in Britain with my parents [kinsfolk], and they welcomed me as a son."[1] That "after a few years" evidently referred to the time since he left Britain in the raiders' boats. At that point in Patrick's story, it couldn't possibly have been "a few years" since he left Ireland. Whatever the case, he was received as a son upon his return.

The phrase "my parents" is a translation of the Latin *parentibus*, which may mean parents, but not necessarily. The fact that these people received Patrick "*as* a son" may suggest that the relatives were not his parents; it would be redundant to say that parents welcomed their own son "as a son." Whoever they were, Patrick's family probably never expected to see him again. In their joy they said the sort of things one would expect them to say. As Patrick phrased it, "[They] asked me, in faith, that after the great tribulations I had endured, I should not go anywhere else away from them."[2]

It is a touching scene of domestic happiness—and it is shattered in the very next line:

> And, of course, there, in a vision of the night, I saw a man whose name was Victoricus coming as if from Ireland with innumerable letters, and he gave me one of them, and I read the beginning of the letter: "The Voice of the Irish"; and as I was reading the beginning of the letter I seemed at that moment to hear the voice of those who were beside the forest of Foclut which is near the western sea, and they were crying as if with one voice: "We beg you, holy youth, that you shall come and shall walk again among us." And I was stung intensely in my heart so that I could read no more.[3]

Consider for a moment the hardships Patrick had just escaped in Ireland. Think of what he suffered as he made his escape. Now he was being called upon to turn around and go back. The vision may not have come as immediately after Patrick's return as it comes in the *Confession*, but for most former slaves, any time would be too soon to return to the place of their enslavement. If Patrick felt any hesitation about returning to Ireland, however, he didn't mention it. He set about making the dream a reality.

Patrick's "Voice of the Irish" dream is one of the best-known episodes in his biography. But there are actually two dreams associated with his call back to Ireland. The second tells quite a lot about Patrick's sense of self, and his particular insecurities. In the first dream, Patrick heard the voice of simple country folk living by the Wood of Fochoill. In the second, he heard the voices of the highly educated, and he couldn't make sense of a word they were saying: "[In] most [learned] words . . . I heard [those whom I] could not understand."[4]

The way back to Ireland would lead Patrick first through training for the priesthood. Judging from the way these two visions play out—and from Patrick's almost obsessive concern with his own lack of education—it was priestly training, not Ireland, that held real terror for Patrick.

In the "learned words" vision, Christ quickly intervened to reassure Patrick. Note the parallels between this vision and the night Satan pressed down on Patrick like a stone:

> [In] most [learned] words . . . I heard [those whom I] could not understand except at the end of the speech it was represented thus: "He who gave his life for you, he it is who speaks within you." And thus I awoke, joyful.
>
> And on a second occasion I saw Him praying within me, and I was as it were, inside my own body, and I heard Him above me—that is, above my inner self. He was praying powerfully with sighs. And in the course of this I was astonished and wondering, and I pondered who it could be who was praying within me. But at the end of the prayer it was revealed to me that it was the Spirit. And so I awoke and

remembered the Apostle's words: "Likewise the Spirit helps us in our weakness; for we know not how to pray as we ought. But the Spirit Himself intercedes for us with sighs too deep for utterance." And again: "The Lord our advocate intercedes for us."[5]

In Patrick's helplessness, the Son of God showed up and reassured him that he, Christ, was at work—it didn't matter if Patrick didn't know what words to say, or even what words other people were saying. God works through weak vessels: here is the truth that kept Patrick moving forward.

The reassurance Patrick got in this dream was the very same that he received on the night Satan attacked him: "It is not you who speaks but the Spirit of your Father speaking in you."[6] It is remarkable that Patrick needed reminding of that truth, not when faced with the prospect of returning to the Irish barbarians, but upon the realization that he was to be among the "learned."

In Patrick's defense, though he was at least twenty-two at the time, his educational attainments would have been at most those of a sixteen-year-old. If he felt educationally inferior to the people with whom he would study for the priesthood, he had good reason. The truly surprising thing is the extent to which that feeling of inferiority was expressed in the pieces Patrick wrote in middle age.

Both the *Confession* and the *Epistle* begin with self-deprecation that goes well beyond the conventional and seems to reflect genuine self-consciousness. In the first line of the *Epistle* Patrick described himself as "unlearned."[7] He was addressing pirates and slave traders, by the way; surely he didn't need to be too self-conscious about his scholarship. The *Confession* begins, "I, Patrick, a sinner, a most simple countryman, the least of all the faithful and most contemptible to many . . ."[8] Patrick's awareness of his inadequacy had been paralyzing. "For some time I have thought of writing," he said, "but I have hesitated until now, for truly, I feared to expose myself to the criticism of men, because I have not studied like others."[9] And that is just the tip of the iceberg. He devoted a good five paragraphs to analyzing the implications of his ignorance on the churchmen who were his original audience.

Patrick eventually settled on an appropriately humble tone, but for a paragraph or two he bounced around between self-loathing, defensiveness, and unseemly suggestions that other people had just had it easier than he did. They had "assimilated both Law and the Holy Scriptures equally and . . . never changed their idiom since their infancy."[10] Some of his fellow churchmen, it seems, came out of the womb speaking (and, apparently, writing) the most high-flown academic Latin. But not Patrick. "My idiom and language have been translated into a foreign tongue . . . It is easy to prove from a sample of my writing."[11] Latin was Patrick's native tongue, but his vernacular Latin would have been quite different from the academic Latin to which he was referring. The Latin of the academics truly would be an alien language to one—even a native Latin speaker—who had never been trained by a rhetor. And that rhetoric phase of education is exactly what Patrick missed in the years of his enslavement.

On top of that, the churchmen of Ireland probably spoke less Latin in day-to-day conversation than the churchmen in Britain and Gaul. Patrick was recruiting priests and monks from the native population in Ireland, and Latin would have been a foreign language for those people. They would have said the Mass in Latin, of course, but Patrick's ecclesiastical Latin may have otherwise grown rusty. He was correct in saying that his academic shortcomings could be proven by the flavor of his writing. Latin experts point out errors and infelicities throughout Patrick's writings, and even in translation there are places where it is clear that Patrick's writing is a little clumsy.

R. P. C. Hanson speaks of Patrick as "acutely, perpetually, embarrassingly conscious of his lack of education."[12] It becomes almost equally embarrassing for the reader as Patrick continues: "So, consequently, today I feel ashamed and am mightily afraid to expose my ignorance, because, [not] eloquent, with a small vocabulary, I am unable to explain as the spirit is eager to do and as the soul and the mind indicate."[13] Now, at last, toward the end of that quotation, Patrick seems to have gotten his rhetorical legs. This was not only a matter of pride or class-consciousness. Patrick felt the frustration of a stutterer. He had so much going on inside—so much desire, so much heart—but his language just couldn't keep up.

That is where Patrick's weakness became his strength. He

testified to the works of God not because he was eloquent (and therefore worthy of praise), but because he couldn't help it. He was "an epistle of Christ," bringing salvation "to the ends of the earth," and written on the hearts of his hearers, "not with ink but with the Spirit of the living God."[14] The apostle Paul wrote similarly that God had sent him to preach the gospel—but "not with words of human wisdom, lest the cross of Christ be emptied of its power" (1 Corinthians 1:17). When he was not wallowing in self-loathing, Patrick realized that his very in-eloquence was what made his message compelling, for it made it clear that *God* had something to say. That is the meaning of his dream of the "learned words." When we don't know what to say, God begins to speak.

Patrick took not just comfort, but confidence from the fact that God uses the foolish things of the world to shame the wise:

> Therefore be amazed, you great and small who fear God, and you men of God, eloquent speakers, listen and contemplate. Who was it summoned me, a fool, from the midst of those who appear wise and learned in the law and powerful in rhetoric and in all things? Me, truly wretched in this world, he inspired before others that I could be—if I would—such a one who, with fear and reverence, and faithfully, without complaint, would come to the people to whom the love of Christ brought me and gave me in my lifetime, if I should be worthy, to serve them truly and with humility.[15]

Why did God use Patrick to reach the people at the very ends of the earth? Because Patrick was sufficiently humble to serve the very barbarians whom the more sophisticated churchmen of his day wanted nothing to do with—and he was sufficiently rustic to relate to them. Whether or not Patrick understood this when he was first called back to Ireland, he clearly understood that Christ would be with him, praying on his behalf and answering his own prayers. So he moved forward.

～

Patrick wrote virtually nothing about his training for the priesthood. There were no seminaries in the fifth century, so he would have trained under a bishop in a mentor setting, though not one-on-one; there would have been other young men receiving instruction at the same time. In the absence of other evidence, it would seem apparent that he trained in Britain. The fact that his father and grandfather were both connected to the British church increases that likelihood. The later legends, however, often have him training in Gaul under Bishop Germanus of Auxerre; that, too is a reasonable possibility.

Of the Patrician legends set in this period of Patrick's training, one of the most interesting is recorded in Jocelin's *Life and Acts*, under the title, "Of the Flesh-meat turned into Fishes." Patrick is a young monk in this story, and he has shown tremendous promise, fasting longer, mortifying the flesh more faithfully, and otherwise outstripping his peers in virtue. God is pleased with him, and, desiring to raise Patrick to positions of high leadership in the Church, has decided to help Patrick grow in humility, so that he might bear with the weak and be more firmly grounded.

The Lord gives the fasting saint a craving for meat. Unable to resist, Patrick finds some pork and hides it away so he can eat it later without drawing notice. He has just left the hiding place when a strange man appears before him with eyes both in the front of his head and in the back. "Who are you?" Patrick asks the man, "and why do you have eyes before and eyes behind?"

The man answers, "I am the servant of God. With the eyes fixed in my forehead I behold the things that are open to view, and with the eyes that are fixed in the hinder part of my head I behold a monk hiding flesh-meat in a vessel, that he may satisfy his appetite [in secret]." Then he disappears.

Cut to the heart, Patrick beats his breast and throws himself to the ground, crying as if guilty of all crimes. But then his guardian angel, Victor, appears in his usual form (apparently the many-eyed man had been Victor in disguise) and tells Patrick to be comforted, to put away his sin, and to mend his ways. Patrick swears off all meat-eating for the rest of his life. But he also asks for a sign to show that he is really forgiven. So the angel tells Patrick to bring the offending meat and plunge it into water. When he does, the pieces of meat come out fish!

Jocelin's scolding coda is the best part of the story. He wrote that many Irish wrongfully misunderstand the miracle. Since Saint Patrick's Day always falls during Lent, some revelers, he said, are inclined "to plunge flesh-meats into water, when plunged in to take out, when taken out to dress, when dressed to eat, and call them fishes of St. Patrick. But hereby every religious man will learn to restrain his appetite, and not to eat meat at forbidden seasons, little regarding what ignorant and foolish men are wont to do."[16]

This story sums up Patrick's character: he was very pious but very human, and the story's comic reversal—indeed, the whole story—hinges on the fact that Patrick was beloved of heaven.

~

Patrick's path toward the post of bishop would have been a long one. If he began his training at twenty-two or twenty-three, it would have been seven or eight years before he was even appointed a deacon (thirty was the minimum age for a deacon). He would have been a priest some years after that, and he was probably no younger than fifty when he was appointed bishop. It is impossible to tell from Patrick's writings whether he went back to Ireland before or after he was appointed bishop.

The legends all portray Patrick as already being a bishop when he comes back to Ireland. Yet given the tremendous amount he accomplished in Ireland, it seems more likely that he started working there as a younger man, before he became bishop.

There is a popular notion that Saint Patrick was the first person to bring Christianity to Ireland. It isn't true. That honor probably belongs to slave traders, like the ones who carried

Patrick into captivity. Of the "thousands" of Britons who, according to Patrick, came to Ireland as slaves, many would have been Christians. As those Christians had children and perhaps converted some of the Irish with whom they had dealings, the Christian population would have grown. Merchants sailing back and forth between Ireland and the Continent and Britain might also have added to the small number of Christians in Ireland in the first decades of the fifth century. By 431, there were enough believers in Ireland that Pope Celestine gave them their own bishop.

There is another popular notion that Saint Patrick was the first bishop of Ireland. That's not true either. It was really a man named Palladius. We don't know much at all about his career in Ireland. In Prosper of Aquitane's *Chronicle*, an entry under 431 simply reads, "Palladius was ordained by Pope Celestine and sent to the Irish believers in Christ as their first bishop."[17] That is the last we hear of Palladius in the historical record.

It seems that Palladius had already made a name for himself as a culture warrior, taking a stand against the spread of the Pelagian heresy in Britain. Pelagius, for whom the heresy was named, was himself of British birth, though he had left for Rome by AD 390. He denied Original Sin and taught that human beings were perfectible, and his heresy was a very hot topic in Patrick's era. In 429 Palladius, then a deacon, convinced Pope Celestine to send the bishop Germanus of Auxerre (the same Germanus who, according to tradition, trained Patrick) to put Britain back on the straight and narrow. According to Prosper,

Germanus "routed the heretics and directed the Britons to the Catholic faith."[18]

Palladius was a bit of a problem for Patrick's hagiographers, such as Muirchu moccu Machtheni, who wrote in the seventh century. Muirchu was writing the biography of the man who brought Christianity to Ireland, and yet he had read Prosper's *Chronicles* and knew that Ireland's first bishop was Palladius. More to the point, he knew that other readers knew it too.

Since he couldn't make Palladius disappear, Muirchu made him irrelevant. Sure, Palladius was appointed bishop, but he wasn't God's man for the job, so he washed out quickly, leaving the post open for Patrick: "Palladius . . . had been consecrated and sent to be established in this island of wintry cold in order to convert it. But no one can receive from earth what has not been given by heaven: Palladius was denied success. For these wild and obdurate people did not readily accept his doctrine and he himself did not wish to spend a long time in a foreign country, but to return to him who had sent him."[19]

Palladius, in Muirchu's version, ended up in Britain and died shortly thereafter. The post open, Patrick gladly filled it. So, by Muirchu's reckoning, Patrick wasn't technically Ireland's first bishop, but he was still the man who brought Christianity to the island. Palladius's term was just a blip, if that. The traditional view came to be that Palladius was appointed in 431 and Patrick in 432.

Patrick did not become a bishop in 432. If for no other reason, he was too young. He couldn't have been much more than forty by then, and he might have been much younger. It is entirely possible that he came to Ireland that early, however. Palladius would have needed a staff, and a young priest or deacon who had lived in Ireland, spoke Irish, and actually wanted to go to Ireland would have been an obvious candidate.

≈

There is one other topic we should cover before we delve into Patrick's career in Ireland. Patrick gave a convoluted account of a humiliating incident in which he was tried by his elders and found wanting. "I was attacked by a goodly number of my elders, who [brought up] my sins against my arduous episcopate,"[20] he wrote. The phrase "arduous episcopate" is vague: does it refer to Patrick's labors in working *toward becoming* a bishop, or to his labors *in the position of* bishop? In other words, was this trial connected to a first, unsuccessful bid for a bishopric, or was Patrick being censured after he had become a bishop? We will assume the former—that Patrick was humiliated the first time he was up for bishop. Patrick was in trouble with his elders when he wrote the *Confession*. The trial of which he was speaking here was clearly a separate incident. He seems to have had a history of run-ins with his elders.

The incident hinges on a betrayal by Patrick's "close friend."[21] We discussed Patrick's boyhood sin—possibly homicide—in chapter 1. To review, he confessed his offense to a friend, most likely a fellow priest-in-training, many years later, before becoming a deacon. Thirty years later (whether thirty years after the sin or thirty years after the confession is unclear), when Patrick's elders sought an occasion against him, his old friend obliged them. He dredged up the old sin that Patrick had confessed in confidence and, as he put it, "in the anxiety [of] my sorrowful mind."[22]

Apparently it was just what Patrick's enemies needed. He wasn't even present for the trial, which took place in Britain. Apparently he expected his friend to plead his case in his absence. The friend reassured Patrick that everything was going to be all right: "See, the rank of bishop goes to you," he said. But during the trial things didn't go as Patrick had expected. The friend, it seems, turned state's evidence. Patrick asks, "How did it come to him, shortly afterwards, to disgrace me publicly, in the presence of all, good and bad, because previously, gladly and of his own free will, he pardoned me, as did the Lord, who is greater than all?"[23]

Reproved by the elders, Patrick was subjected to "disgrace and scandal."[24] In the middle of his public humiliation and private pain, God came to Patrick again in a dream. In this dream Patrick saw the official document of censure that had been drawn up against him. Then he heard the voice of God: "We have seen with displeasure the face of the chosen one divested of [his good] name . . . He who touches you, touches the apple [i.e., pupil] of my eye."[25]

This is a remarkable moment. The antiauthoritarian theme that runs throughout Patrick's writings is crystallized in this image: the document of censure, that artifact of the Church hierarchy held in front of Patrick's face, is nullified by God himself with a direct word that short-circuits the whole apparatus of church leadership. God sides with Patrick against his elders. And if God is for him, who can be against him?

This confidence empowered Patrick to show magnanimity toward those who had (in his mind, at least) attacked and persecuted him. "I pray God that it shall not be held against them as a sin that I fell truly into disgrace and scandal," he said.[26] As for the friend who betrayed him, Patrick grieved for the broken relationship with one "to whom," he said, "I entrusted my soul."[27] Yet even after being handed over by this man, Patrick still referred to him, in the very same paragraph, as "my very close friend."

Rather than growing bitter, Patrick came out with a renewed commitment to the work that God had called him to. Throughout his career, Patrick trusted his direct line to God more than he trusted the leadership of his superiors. This attitude would be a source of ongoing trouble for Patrick (including the trouble that led to his writing the *Confession*); but without it, he would have never begun the work of bringing the Irish to Christ.

5

"AMONG BARBAROUS TRIBES"

W hen Patrick finally made it back to Ireland, what did his work there look like? In the legends, the triumph of the gospel is a foregone conclusion. Muirchu tells of two druids in the service of the great king Loiguire who had warned of Patrick's coming with "a foreign tradition, a new form of rule as it were, with a strange and troublesome doctrine brought from far beyond the sea. A few would proclaim it; many would accept it; all would honor it; it would overthrow kingdoms; kill the kings who resisted; subvert the common people; and destroy all their gods; and, having cast aside all the works of their culture, it would rule forever."[1]

Of Patrick himself, the druids said:

Adze-head will come, with his curve-head stick;
He will chant wicked incantations from his gap-headed house,

From his table in the front end of the house;
All his household will answer, "so be it, so be it."[2]

Patrick's arrival, according to the legends, looked more like a victory lap than the beginning of a long, slow mission. A dog sent to attack him went as stiff as a stone (showing the locals what happens to those who worship stones). A man sent to attack him likewise found himself unable to move, "And he, experiencing in himself such a miracle, suddenly is changed into another man, and from proud becoming humble, mild from fierce, from an infidel a believer, he is, with all his household, at the preaching of Patrick, baptized in the Christian faith."[3]

In the legends, everybody Patrick came in contact with was in grave danger of getting converted on the spot. One of the most fascinating of the stories tells of Patrick's efforts to reunite with his former master, Miliucc. As *The Tripartite Life* puts it, Patrick "thought fit as he labored at first for his body, that he should labor for his soul."[4] He took along some gold with which to prevail on Miliucc to believe, remembering that Miliucc "was covetous regarding gold."[5]

Miliucc, for his part, had heard how people converted to Christianity when they spoke with Patrick, and he wanted none of it. He considered it beneath him to submit to the teachings of a man who had once been his slave. And yet he had heard that Patrick could be extremely compelling. He was afraid that his former slave's preaching would penetrate his stony heart, or that some undeniable miracle would compel him to believe.

When a servant reported to Miliucc that the holy man was nearby, Miliucc "went into his royal house with his gold and silver; and he set the house on fire, and was burned with all his treasures, and his soul went to hell."[6] At least he died doing what he loved best.

It is hard to believe Patrick's mission to the Irish—the historical rather than the legendary one—could have gotten off to such a roaring start. There is nothing in Patrick's writings to indicate that the Irish had been so obliging. In the *Confession* he specifically declined to offer a play-by-play account of his ministry. "It [would be] tedious to describe in detail all my labours one by one," he said,[7] though the reader would be glad for a few more details than Patrick offered. From the *Confession* and the *Epistle* together, however, we can glean enough details to have a broad outline of his work.

Patrick spoke of his return to Ireland as a voluntary re-enslavement. "Could I have come to Ireland without thought of God, merely in my own interest?" he asked in the *Letter*. "Who was it made me come? For here I am a 'prisoner of the Spirit' so that I may not see any of my family."[8] He was creating a parallel with Paul here, who often spoke of himself as a "prisoner of Christ" (Ephesians 3:1; see also Ephesians 4:1; 2 Timothy 1:8; Philemon 1:1, 9).

Unlike his first tour of duty in Ireland, this time Patrick's servitude was voluntary. When Patrick finally went back to Ireland, there were people who didn't understand, his family among them. Of his departure, he said, "Many gifts were offered to me with weeping and tears, and I offended them [the donors] and also went against the wishes of a good number of my elders; but guided by God, I neither agreed with them nor deferred to them."[9] There is Patrick in a nutshell: guided by God, he neither agreed with his critics nor deferred to them, no matter how good their intentions. He burned with a passion that would not be suppressed so that, he wrote:

> I might come to the Irish people to preach the Gospel and endure insults from unbelievers; that I might hear scandal of my travels, and endure many persecutions to the extent of prison; and so that I might give up my free birthright for the advantage of others, and if I should be worthy, I am ready [to give] even my life without hesitation; and most willingly for His name. And I choose to devote it to him even unto death, if God grant it to me.[10]

That's a very different man from the conqueror portrayed in the legends, who goes from victory to victory, hardly stopping for a breather. He remarked elsewhere in the *Epistle* that some of the Irish still look down on him. Perhaps more of them were able to resist Patrick's eloquence than the legends would have us believe.

Nevertheless, Patrick made it clear that he did experience incredible success as an evangelist in Ireland: "I am greatly God's debtor, because he granted me so much grace, that through me many people would be reborn in God, and soon . . .

after confirmed, and that clergy would be ordained everywhere for them, the masses lately come to belief, whom the Lord drew from the ends of the earth . . . and shall say, 'Our fathers have inherited naught but lies, worthless things in which there is no profit.'"[11]

Masses lately come to belief. More than that, *clergy ordained.* All from people whose fathers inherited (and bequeathed) nothing but pagan lies. In another place Patrick wrote that he baptized "so many thousands of people."[12] No one had ever done what Patrick was doing in Ireland. Never before had a Catholic clergyman gone out among the pagans and made mass conversions. How, exactly, did he do it?

Patrick's efforts don't appear to have been entirely grass-roots. He cultivated relationships with kings and their families. This would have been wise on the simple grounds that he couldn't have traveled safely in Ireland without the friendship—or at least the permission—of the petty kings. And Patrick's program included a great deal of travel. "I went about among you, and everywhere for your sake," he said, "in danger, and as far as the outermost regions beyond which no one lived, and where no one had ever penetrated before, to baptize or to ordain clergy or to confirm people."[13]

Bribery was part of the program too. "From time to time I gave rewards to the kings, as well as making payments to their sons who travel with me."[14] Those kings' sons would have been bodyguards who protected Patrick as he traveled from tuatha to tuatha. Or perhaps "protection racket" would be a more fitting term. In one incident he described of his travels with his royal bodyguards, things went bad. It is not clear whether the kings' sons attacked him or simply failed to protect him from attackers:

> Notwithstanding which, they seized me with my companions, and that day most avidly desired to kill me. But my time had not yet come. They plundered everything they found on us anyway, and fettered me in irons; and on the fourteenth day the Lord freed me from their power, and whatever they had of ours was given back to us for the sake of God on account of the indispensable friends whom we had made before.[15]

A rough business, this evangelism. Everywhere he went, Patrick was subject to the whims of some powerful man or another. In this scene, when one set of strongmen turns on him, it is the influence of other strongmen who get him out of the jam. It's a good thing he had cultivated those "indispensable friends." Jesus instructed his disciples to be as "wise as serpents and innocent as doves" (Matthew 10:16 ESV). The advice was equally appropriate for Patrick. He seemed to have learned a thing or two about navigating the patchwork politics of fifth-century Ireland.

In several places Patrick said he would count it an honor to be martyred for the cause of Christ. That wasn't just a vague notion, but a very real possibility. For all his success in making converts, it is clear that he was not universally beloved in

Ireland. For that matter, it was his success that caused much of the danger. In failure or in passivity he would hardly have attracted the notice of the powerful.

Patrick also mentioned the fact that he had to pay off "those who were administering justice in all the regions, which," he wrote, "I visited often."[16] He had paid out the price of fifteen men and was still paying. Where did all the money for these bribes come from?[17] Perhaps at least some of it came from Patrick's own pocket. When he said, "I have sold this nobility of mine,"[18] he may have been speaking literally. Maybe he sold the family farm, or part of it, to finance his mission in Ireland. We don't know exactly "the price of fifteen men," but if he meant the price of a slave, which seems likely, that would have been a huge sum of money. And that was only part of the expense of which he spoke. Unless he sold a very large birthright, it seems unlikely that he would have been able to finance his whole operation out of his own pocket.

It is more likely that the British church financed Patrick's work in Ireland. If so, it is not hard to imagine there being some friction. A renegade bishop asking for vast sums of money to finance a mission to the most murderous sort of barbarians? And much of that money to pay bribes? To borrow a catchphrase from the modern church, it raises questions about good stewardship.

Yet Patrick's interactions with Irish kings and their families yielded more than safe passage. In some cases they yielded converts. "So, how is it that in Ireland," he wrote, "where they never had any knowledge of God but, always, until now, cherished idols and unclean things, they are lately become a people of the Lord, and are called children of God? The sons of the Irish [Scotti] and the daughters of the chieftains are to be seen as monks and virgins of Christ."[19]

It is an amazing thing when those who have the most to lose (in earthly terms) throw it away for the sake of a new religion! It may be significant, however, that Patrick mentioned no chieftains converting, only their children.

Liam de Paor suggests that the Irish kings' raiding and looting of Roman lands may have helped open them to the Roman religion that Patrick brought. He wrote, "They may have originally chopped up ornate Roman dinner services [from their looting] merely for the silver of which they were made, indifferent to the répoussé Cupids, Baccae, vines and peacocks with which they were adorned; but soon, in their own way, they learned to emulate Roman fashions."[20] That's a striking image—the barbarian warlord, about to throw a silver spoon into the smelter, but then suddenly arrested by the beauty and intricacy of its craftsmanship. As he stays his hand, admiring the spoon, he begins to wonder what sort of world could produce such a thing. And then an emissary from that world shows up in the person of Patrick. We often speak of Patrick as bringing to Ireland a faith that was no longer exclusively Roman. But it is possible that in certain quarters his Roman credentials were a selling point.

For the most part Patrick spoke of his Irish converts collectively; the one individual he mentioned was "a most beautiful, blessed, native-born noble Irish [Scotta] woman of adult age whom," he said, "I baptized." A few days after her baptism, this woman said that she had received a prophecy advising her to become a "virgin of Christ." Six days later, "she took the course that all virgins of God take, not with their fathers' consent but enduring the persecutions and deceitful hindrances of their parents."[21]

A king with a beautiful daughter would expect to benefit from her marriage. A good marriage was an excellent way for him to make alliances, increase his fortune, and consolidate his power. Quite apart from the usual shock of having a daughter announce that she is devoting herself entirely to a novel religion, the land-owning parents of a "virgin of Christ" would have had a whole other portfolio of concerns. The pressures on such a young woman would have been tremendous.

The problem, from the parents' perspective, is summed up nicely by a king in one of the Patrick legends whose daughter decided to become a virgin for Christ: "I had determined that my daughter should continue unto me a long-descending progeny for the confirmation of my kingdom and the solace of mine age; but the succession is cut off, and mine hope is defeated by thee."[22]

The plight of Patrick's pious noblewoman fired the imagination of storytellers in the Patrician tradition. There are several legends in which the beautiful daughters of kings refuse marriage for the sake of God and are punished by their parents. In these stories women demonstrate not just moral strength but a level of self-determination not typically available to women in their culture. The best known is the story of Monesan from Muirchu's *Life*. In her pursuit of truth, Monesan chooses virginity and stands firm in spite of all: "The more she was wet through with drenchings of water, the less she could be compelled against her will. Indeed, between floggings and dowsings with water, she still contrived to ask her mother and her nurse if they knew who made the wheel with which the world is provided with light."[23]

Throughout the history of Christianity, women have been "early adopters," typically leading the men in embracing the faith when it spreads to a new area. Not surprisingly, women played an important role in the work of the missionary Patrick, and he showed remarkable concern and tenderness toward the women under his spiritual care. He demonstrated a special compassion for those virgins who were slaves, and therefore had no control over their own virginity: "Those who are kept in slavery suffer the most," he wrote. "They endure terrors and constant threats, but the Lord has given grace to many of his handmaidens, for even though they are forbidden to do so, still they resolutely follow his example."[24] In the next chapter we will look more closely at the fate of some of Patrick's female converts who were carried into slavery by the warlord Coroticus.

≈

While Patrick cultivated relationships with the rich and powerful, it is clear from his writing that his evangelism did not hinge on influence peddling. He was a pastor, a shepherd, first and last, and the road was not always easy: "After hardships and such great trials," he rejoiced, "after captivity, after many years, he [has given] me so much favour in these people."[25] He found favor with them because he showed them a respect that they might not have expected from a representative of the civilized world. "[To] the heathen among whom I live," he said, "I have shown them trust and have always shown them trust."[26] That must have been a remarkable thing for the people he served, especially considering that he had once been an involuntary slave to the Irish and had learned firsthand how dangerous they could be.

In a culture of violence, Patrick brought a message of peace. In a civilization known for boasting, he brought an arresting humility. And in a world of arbitrary pagan gods, Patrick brought the message of a personal God who loves his people, even to the extremity of losing his life. In fact, Patrick would have been happy to be martyred for the sake of Christ and his beloved Irish. What he couldn't bear was the thought of being parted from those he was sent to serve. "May it never befall me to be separated by my God from his people whom he has won in this most remote land. I pray God that he gives me perseverance, and that he will deign that I should be a faithful witness for his sake right up to the time of my passing."[27]

In his writings, Patrick comes across as a man who has been transformed by the knowledge that God loves him, who doesn't need the trappings of the world to give meaning to his life. For example, in one of the many legends in which he does battle with the druids upon his return to Ireland as a missionary, a great landowner named Dairé has been quarreling with him over a piece of hilltop land that Patrick asked for. Remorseful, Dairé brings Patrick a marvelous imported triple-sized cauldron as a kind of peace offering. On receiving the cauldron, Patrick simply says, "*Graʒacham*" (apparently a corruption of the Latin *gratias agimus*, or "we give thanks").

As Dairé goes home, he grows dissatisfied with the exchange. "This man is a fool," he says, "who can find nothing better to say than '*Graʒacham*' for such a marvelous cauldron of triple measure." So he sends his servants to take the cauldron back. When the servants take the cauldron, Patrick simply says, "*Graʒacham*. Take it."

When the servants get home with the cauldron, Dairé questions them:

> "What did the Christian say when you repossessed the cauldron?"
>
> They answered: "He said '*Graʒacham*.'"
>
> Dairé responded to this, saying, "'*Graʒacham*' for the giving. '*Graʒacham*' for the taking away. His saying is so good that for these '*Graʒachams*' the cauldron will be brought back to him again."

And Dairé himself came long this time and bore the cauldron to Patrick, saying to him, "Let this cauldron now be yours. You are a stubborn and imperturbable man.

Furthermore, I now give you that piece of land that you pre-viously asked for—in so far as it is mine. Live there." And that is the city now called Armagh.[28]

Graʒacham for the giving, *Graʒacham* for the taking away. Patrick had learned to be content in all things.

There is something compelling about the stubborn gratitude and equanimity that Patrick's enslavement nurtured in him. He had been imprisoned, robbed, threatened, and mocked. He'd been betrayed by his dearest friend and punished by a church hierarchy that didn't get him. As he wrote the *Confession*, he was in trouble again. "I certainly am wretched and unfortunate," he said. "Even if I wanted wealth I have no resources . . . Daily I expect to be murdered or betrayed or reduced to slavery if the occasion arises." And yet, in spite of all, he wrote, "But I see that even here and now, I have been exalted beyond measure by the Lord . . . [Besides,] poverty and failure suit me better than wealth and delight." Why? Because, he affirmed, "Christ the Lord was poor for our sakes."[29]

Patrick must have looked like Christ to the people of Ireland. Like the Savior, he lowered himself for their sake, giv-ing up his rights and privileges, to willingly serve where he might have been served. No amount of eloquence could make the same impact.

6

COROTICUS

Of Patrick's writings, his *Letter to the Soldiers of Coroticus* is the one in which his pastoral spirit is most evident. Ironically, that pastoral tenderness finds expression in hot-burning anger against men who have grievously wronged a group of Patrick's beloved converts.

Coroticus was a British warlord, one of the petty tyrants who came to power throughout Britain in the years after the Roman army left. Coroticus is the Latinized form of the British name Ceretic. Two tyrants named Ceretic appear in the fifth-century historical record, one based in Wales, the other in Scotland. It is not clear from the evidence which (if either) of these was Patrick's Coroticus.

What we do know of Coroticus is that he directed a raid on the Irish coast in which a group of freshly baptized Christian converts were attacked; some were killed and some were carried back to Britain as slaves. The Irish victims were so freshly baptized, in fact, that they were still wearing their white baptismal robes, and the chrism was still shining on their foreheads. The visual is striking: the new Christians in their pure white robes—then the confusion and terror and blood wrought by sword-wielding pirates.

The irony wouldn't have been lost on Patrick. Just as he had been carried from Britain to Ireland by Irish raiders, now, decades later, members of his flock had been carried across the Irish Sea in the other direction, by British raiders.

But there was another irony at work here—an uglier irony. Coroticus wasn't a pagan warlord descending on Christian victims. He was himself a professing Christian. We have seen already that Christianity was the religion of the ruling class in Patrick's Britain. Coroticus, in fact, may have come from a family background similar to Patrick's, since the decurion class would have given rise to many of Britain's local tyrants. It is not as strange as it may at first sound for a British warlord to be a nominal Christian. The thought of a Christian conducting piratical raids on anyone was horrifying enough, but to think he would prey on fellow Christians was more than Patrick could bear.

As soon as he heard about the raid, Patrick sent a priest to Coroticus's soldiers bearing a letter, "to see," he said, "if we might claw something back from all the looting, most important, the baptized captives whom they had seized."[1] The soldiers laughed in the priest's face.

The epistle we know as *A Letter to the Soldiers of Coroticus* is a second letter, not the first one that the priest delivered directly. It is an open letter; Patrick evidently distributed multiple copies in the hopes that "whosoever is a servant of God . . . be a willing bearer of this letter." Patrick directed the reader to read the letter out loud "before all the people in the presence of Coroticus himself."[2]

The *Letter*, or *Epistle* (see introduction), is a document of excommunication, though Patrick would have had no official authority to excommunicate a Christian belonging to a British diocese. But, as was typical of Patrick, he believed his authority came directly from God, not from a church hierarchy. His letter was a rebuke not only to Coroticus and his men, but also to the leadership of the British church, who, Patrick was convinced, didn't care enough about their fellow Christians in Ireland to do anything about the depredations of a British Christian against them.

Patrick's self-introduction is a three-sentence capsule of the self-image that he projected throughout his writings: "I, Patrick, a sinner and unlearned, have been appointed a bishop in Ireland, and I accept from God what I am. I dwell amongst barbarians as a proselyte and a fugitive for the love of God. He will testify that it is so."[3]

He led with humility, calling himself both a sinner and unlearned. And yet his authority to speak was genuine—he was a bishop, but even more important than a title bestowed by men was the fact that *God* had made him so. For the love of God, he said, he lived among barbarous tribes (was this a little dig at Coroticus, who had been far more barbarous than the barbarians?). Then the classic Patrician flourish: God himself will testify that this is so. Without fail, Patrick drew his authority directly from the Divine, without any human intervention.

Patrick was moved to write, he said, by zeal for God and "by love of my neighbors who are my only sons."[4] Those people whom Coroticus had murdered and enslaved meant everything to Patrick: for them, he wrote, "I have forsaken my country and parents, and would give up even life itself."[5] The page burns with Patrick's passion for the people of Ireland. They were the only offspring he would ever have.

The Irish believers were no longer foreigners to Patrick, but fellow citizens. The British soldiers, on the other hand, Patrick's countrymen and supposedly his brothers in Christ, were no such thing. "I am not addressing my own people," Patrick said, "nor my fellow citizens of the holy Romans, but those who are now become citizens of demons by reason of their evil works."[6] Patrick was hinting at excommunication with this language. These allegedly Christian soldiers weren't simply off track. To Patrick's eyes, they had left the kingdom of God and had proven to be under Satan's authority.

It is interesting and a little surprising that Patrick used "Scots" and "Picts" as terms of abuse. Yet he wrote that Coroticus and his men were "companions of the apostate Scots and Picts, blood-thirsty men, ever ready to redden themselves with the blood of innocent Christians."[7] Later he would speak of "the wicked, abandoned, and apostate Picts."[8] Patrick had made it his life's work to bring the good news to the Irish, who would themselves have been candidates for the description "wicked, abandoned, and apostate"; in so doing, he demonstrated that even the wickedest apostates aren't necessarily immune to grace. Why, then, did he write off a whole tribe this way? Perhaps he was playing to the prejudices of his British audience, who had built a wall all the way across their island to keep the Picts away. Or, just as likely, perhaps he was revealing his own prejudices. Not even saints are perfectly consistent.

Ever compassionate, and always attentive to the deeper spiritual truth of a situation, Patrick said he couldn't decide whether to weep more for those who were killed or enslaved, or for those who did the killing and enslaving. Those men were the true slaves, he believed. They had chained themselves to the devil himself, for "whoever commits sin is the slave of sin."[9] There is more than one kind of slavery, and as Patrick could attest from personal experience, physical slavery isn't the worst kind.

When Patrick actually articulated the "excommunication" that he'd been hinting at, it was a strange excommunication indeed. He wrote, "Let every man know who fears God that they are estranged from me, and from Christ my God, whose ambassador I am."[10] It is as if the authority to excommunicate began with Patrick and then reached to Christ. "They are estranged *from me*." In his righteous anger, Patrick's confidence in his ability to know God's will directly veered very close to presumption.

Having declared Coroticus and his soldiers to be outcasts, Patrick named the sins for which they were cast out: patricide and fratricide.[11] Fratricide makes sense: they killed their brothers in Christ. But why patricide? Whose father did they kill? Perhaps Patrick was implying that by murdering believers, they were guilty of murdering (or at least attempting to murder) God the Father. Or was he making a pun in reference to his own name? By calling the raiders patricides, he may have been suggesting that they had actually killed *him*, Patrick, or Patricius.

The particular shame of these murders, according to Patrick, was that they had destroyed the work that God had been doing among the Irish. "'The wicked have scattered your law, O Lord,' which in these latter days he had planted in Ireland with so much hope and goodness; here it had been taught and nurtured in God's sight."[12] That mournful language is so beautiful: "so much hope and goodness." It was slow work, requiring careful nurture, and so fragile too.

Part II of the *Epistle* begins with the telling clause "I do not overreach myself."[13] Anytime a person says, "I do not overreach myself," there is a good chance he or she has either just overreached or is about to. Having excommunicated Coroticus and his men, it seems to have occurred to Patrick that he has overreached and needs to explain himself. "I share with these whom He hath called . . . to preach the Gospel . . . even to the ends of the earth."[14] Patrick seemed to be saying that even though Coroticus did not belong to his particular diocese, the crime was still committed in his diocese, because his diocese extended, by virtue of his calling from God, to "the ends of the earth." Therefore, he concluded, he had jurisdiction. It wasn't even a question of a conflict between Coroticus and Patrick anyway, Patrick said. The conflict was between Satan, "who [had] acted invidiously . . . through the tyranny of Coroticus," and God, who had given his priests (including Patrick) "the high divine power, [namely,] 'Whosoever they shall bind on earth shall be bound in heaven.'"[15]

Though he still hadn't used the word *excommunication* (nor would he), Patrick reminded the Christian reader of his responsibilities in the matter of excommunication: "I beseech you, therefore, who are the holy ones of God and humble of heart, that you will not be flattered by [those expelled from the Church], and that you will neither eat nor drink with them, nor receive their alms, until they do penance with many tears, and liberate the servants of God and the baptized hand-maids of Christ."[16]

Excommunication is not strictly punitive. It also has a remedial goal: to make the excommunicant feel what it is to be separated from the fellowship of God and so to turn back to God and to the Church. Patrick added an additional goal to this particular excommunication: to free the kidnapped slaves.

"You will neither eat nor drink with them, nor receive their alms." The second half of this sentence deserves further discussion. Patrick spent so much time expanding on this idea that we have to wonder what he knew that we don't. Paragraph 8, as seen in Skinner's translation, consists entirely of six Bible verses on the subject of ill-gotten gains: "The Almighty turns away the gifts of wicked men. He who offers sacrifice from the goods of the poor, is like a man who sacrifices a son in the sight of his own father,"[17] and on for several more lines. The next paragraph is a discussion on greed and the connection between greed, envy, and murder.

It would seem at first that Patrick was preaching to Coroticus and his men. And no doubt he was. They, after all, were greedy murderers in the story. But he was also preaching to Christians, and likely the church leaders, in Britain. These two preachy paragraphs tie back to the injunction not to receive alms from Coroticus. Perhaps Coroticus—or men like him—had been seeking to buy favor with church leaders by giving large "alms" that were really just bribes. Yes, Coroticus and his men were greedy. But churchmen can be greedy too. Patrick implied that priests are complicit in such men's crimes when they receive the fruits of their misdeeds.

To such self-interested behavior—by Coroticus and perhaps by British churchmen—Patrick contrasted his own disinterested work among the Irish:

Did I come to Ireland according to God or according to the flesh? Who compelled me? I was led by the Spirit, that I should see my relatives no more. Have I not a pious mercy towards that nation which formerly took me captive? According to the flesh, I am of noble birth, my father being a Decurion. I do not regret or blush for having bartered my nobility for the good of others. I am a servant in Christ unto a foreign people

for the ineffable glory of eternal life, which is in Christ Jesus
my Lord.[18]

There may have been a touch of self-congratulation here.
But there was also a new vision for the way the world can work.
Either Patrick was a lunatic, or God had done an incredible
thing. Once a slave under duress, Patrick was now a slave by
choice. At one time a victim of a people who had captured him
and wrecked his father's house, now he had become the bene-
factor of those very people. Clearly Patrick viewed himself as a
slave of Christ, but he also saw himself as belonging to the Irish
people he had come to serve. In the midst of a dark drama of
Coroticus's rampant self-aggrandizement, Patrick offered the
hope of selflessness.

In giving up his old life, Patrick gave up much of his iden-
tity, including, it seems, his Britishness. Over the next couple of
paragraphs, Patrick made some obscure remarks regarding his
reputation in Britain. "My own people do not acknowledge me,"
he said; "'A prophet is without honor in his own country.'"[19]
Perhaps he was referring to the disrespect with which Coroticus
and his men treated his representative; perhaps he expected better treatment on the grounds that he, like Coroticus, was of
British birth. On the other hand, he may have been thinking
about the British church and feeling self-conscious about the
way he was perceived among his former colleagues.

"Who of the saints would not dread to share in the feasts
or amusements of such persons? They fill their houses with the

spoils of the Christian dead,"[20] he said, making it crystal clear that a *good* Christian would never associate with these pirates—which raises the question, did he have reason to believe that some "good Christians" were, in fact, feasting with Coroticus and his band of assassins in their homes—houses filled with the spoils of Christians they had slain? There could be an implied criticism of the British church here; Patrick seemed genuinely concerned that his British brethren were turning a blind eye to Coroticus's crimes.

Patrick admired the Gaulish Christians' approach when their members were carried into slavery: they sent holy, capable men with bags of money to buy them back. Coroticus and his men were doing the exact opposite: when they weren't killing their Christian prisoners, they were selling them into slavery, and in far-off lands that didn't know God. "You might as well consign Christ's own members to a whorehouse," he said; then, in his indignation he spluttered question after question. "What kind of hope can you have left in God? Can you still trust someone who says he agrees with you? Do you listen still to all those flatterers around you?"[21]

Nearing the end of the letter, Patrick let himself mourn his loss:

> I cry out with grief and sorrow. O beautiful and well-beloved brethren and children! whom I have brought forth in Christ in such multitudes, what shall I do for you? . . . The wicked have prevailed over us. We have become outcasts. It would seem

that they do not think we have one baptism and one Father, God. They think it an indignity that we have been born in Ireland; as He said: "Have ye not one God? Why do ye each forsake his neighbor?" Therefore I grieve for you—I grieve, O my beloved ones![22]

Note Patrick's full identification with his people: "*we* have been born in Ireland." He felt the same injustices that they felt. And he resented the fact that the British were treating the Irish as subhuman. They had one God, he said. So why were the Irish Christians still on the outside?

Ever the pastor, Patrick moved from mourning and resentment to comfort and the hope of heaven.

But, on the other hand, I congratulate myself I have not labored for nothing—my journey has not been in vain . . . Thanks be to God, ye who have believed and have been baptized have gone from earth to paradise. Certainly, ye have begun to migrate where there is no night or death or sorrow; but ye shall exult like young bulls loosed from their bonds and tread down the wicked under your feet as dust.

Truly, you shall reign with the apostles and prophets and martyrs, and obtain the eternal kingdom.[23]

It is the grand reversal: the victim has become the victor. The murdered converts, he said, would one day reign on high, while outside "the dogs, and . . . murderers . . . shall have their part in the everlasting lake of fire."[24] Furthermore, he assured them, they would someday sit in judgment of Coroticus and his men!

The penultimate paragraph of the *Letter* provides, once again, a nice summary of Patrick's vision of his own authority. He never put confidence in any cleverness of his own; he actually viewed his academic shortcomings as a confirmation that what he said must be from God: "I bear witness before God and his angels that this will come about, just as he has revealed my lack of learning. To repeat: these are not my words, but God's own words—and the apostles' and the prophets', which I have merely chiseled out in Latin."[25] It's not the sort of stance that invites debate.

Reading Patrick's *Epistle*, it is not hard to see why the Irish loved him. He felt things deeply and wasn't afraid to express a righteous anger. Neither was he afraid to overstep his bounds when he felt he was right or when he was speaking up on behalf of someone who had been wronged. He could be impolitic, but he was a bulldog on behalf of his people. He was a pastor in every sense.

"A WITNESS TO ALL NATIONS"

We could hardly overestimate the uniqueness of Patrick's work among the Irish. As a pioneering missionary, his only real precedent was the apostle Paul. When he took it upon himself to make disciples among the Irish, he became, so far as we know, Western Christendom's first missionary to the world beyond the bounds of the Roman Empire.[1] Paul's journeys were an astonishing achievement, but even Paul never ventured beyond the empire of which he was a citizen. For that matter, Paul's travels rarely took him even a hundred miles away from the Mediterranean Sea, the center of the Roman world. In reconciling Jew and Greek, Paul already had his work cut out for him; the barbarians hardly figured into the equation for him.[2]

For five centuries after Paul's missionary journeys—until Pope Gregory the Great's "Gregorian mission" set out to evangelize Britain's pagan Anglo-Saxons in 596—the barbarians beyond the Roman frontier still didn't figure in the Church's plans, except as foes of the faith. By Patrick's time, a de facto orthodoxy had emerged that conflated Christianity with Roman civilization in much the same way that first-century Jewish Christians assumed that Christian practice would and should be shaped by Jewish cultural mores. For Patrick to reach out to the barbarians as he did was almost as radical as Paul's outreach to the Gentiles.

In its first two centuries, the Christian faith was viewed as a threat to Roman civilization. The empire had typically been quite tolerant of religious differences, happy to let conquered peoples worship whichever deities struck their fancy. Mercury was glad to share the heavens with Diana and with the Celts' Lug and with any other local gods that might have presided over the patchwork of peoples ruled by Rome. What the empire could not very well tolerate, however, was a God that would not share the heavens. Jews and Christians, with their exclusive, monotheistic claims, did not enjoy the same tolerance that other people groups enjoyed.

By the second half of the fourth century, however, the Church had come to be viewed as the guardian and sole guarantor of Roman civilization. In *The World of Late Antiquity*,[3] Peter Brown tells the story of how this remarkable change came about. What follows is a summary (and simplification) of Brown's thesis. Anyone interested in the last centuries of the Roman Empire could do no better than Brown's body of work.

The classical culture of the Mediterranean Basin had always been the epicenter of Roman civilization. But as the Empire expanded beyond the Mediterranean, that classical civilization was slow to follow. The Roman army, after all, moved much more swiftly than the books and arts and traditions of a centuries-old culture. Brown speaks of "inner barbarians"[4] who inhabited places like Gaul—subjects, even citizens of the empire, but outsiders to the civilization that had shaped the empire.

Those "inner barbarians"—at least the ones who aspired to be viewed as Romans rather than barbarians—needed some connection to Roman culture. Christianity became a bridge, or perhaps a shortcut to Romanness for the peoples of the north and west. As Brown puts it, Christianity "had expanded inside the Roman world by loosening the boundary between the 'inner barbarians' of the empire and classical civilization."[5]

In the third and fourth centuries, as "outer barbarians" threatened the empire from the outside, Christian apologists began to make the case that Christianity was the only hope for the survival of the Roman Empire and its culture. According to Brown: "They claimed that Christianity was the sole guarantee of that civilization—that the best traditions of classical philosophy and the high standards of classical ethics could be steeled against barbarism only through being confirmed by Christian revelation; and that the beleaguered Roman empire was saved from destruction only by the protection of the Christian God."[6]

These same apologists taught that for a pagan to convert to Christianity was "to step, at last, from a confused and undeveloped stage of moral and intellectual growth into the heart of civilization."[7]

Constantine the Great, who converted in AD 312, was himself one of those "inner barbarians" for whom Christianity was a bridge to the heart of Roman culture. He grew up in what is now Serbia, far from the heart of the empire. In becoming a Christian, Brown points out, Constantine publicly claimed to be saving the empire. With the zeal of a convert, he set about the work of making Christianity Rome's state religion.[8]

Constantine's work did much to strengthen Christianity throughout the civilized world. By the end of the fourth century, the Church was as big as all the empire—but, it appeared, no bigger. It wasn't obvious whether, in this close association between Church and state, the Church had conquered the empire, or the empire had conquered the Church.

If the Church was Rome's church, then any enemy of the empire was an enemy of the Church. If the Church had never reached out to the "outer barbarians" before Patrick, it wasn't because they simply had never gotten around to it. It was because they didn't see any point. Brown quotes two church officials on the subject: "'What place would God have in a savage world?' wrote one; 'How could the Christian virtues survive among barbarians?' wrote another."[9]

And Patrick's experience as a youth would seem to prove the bishops' point: a boy is snatched away from his Christian home, removed from civilized Christian society, and enslaved in a dark world of paganism and error. Yes, these barbarians are indeed enemies to the gospel.

Those are the prejudices against which Patrick labored. It would take a true renegade—a man who is somewhat suspicious of authority—to do what he did. As we have seen already, when the Church sent Patrick to Ireland, it wouldn't have been so he could convert the barbarians. He would have been sent to minister to the few Christians who were already there.

It appears that Patrick's refusal to go along with the program was the occasion for his writing the *Confession*. He was in self-defense mode in this piece, justifying the work he was doing in Ireland. And the gist of his self-defense, over and over, was that his authority derived directly from God. God spoke to Patrick in dreams, guided him through his passions and desires, and proved that he was at work by protecting Patrick and granting him success. Even Patrick's ignorance and rusticity were proof that he was on a mission from God: how could a bumpkin like him enjoy so much success if God weren't behind him?

"Many were trying to prevent [my] mission," Patrick said. "They were talking among themselves behind my back, and saying: 'Why is this fellow throwing himself into danger among enemies who know not God?' Not from malice, but having no liking for it; likewise, as I myself can testify, they perceived my rusticity."[10]

As Patrick points out, we need not read any malice into the opposition that he experienced. People simply didn't get what he was doing. The "outer barbarians" weren't part of their plan. The Irish knew not God. For Patrick's opponents, that was reason enough to stay away from them. For Patrick, it was exactly why he embraced them.

Apparently there were some clergymen who caught Patrick's vision and agreed with him that he did indeed have the authority to do what he was doing. He spoke of "brethren and co-workers, who . . . believed me because of what I have foretold and still foretell to strengthen and reinforce your faith."[11] He dwelled on his dreams and visions because for him, his ability to foretell the future was the surest evidence of his authority.

But he couldn't help scolding those who still disagreed with him: "I wish only that you, too, would make greater and better efforts."[12] That's a strange thing to say in a document in which a man is addressing superiors who, apparently, are sitting in judgment of him. Patrick comes across in the *Confession* as a man who simply didn't do church politics very well. He comes across as a little naive—rustic, even. Even if Patrick believed his authority derived directly from God and had nothing to do with the Church hierarchy, he might have tried harder to show proper deference for that hierarchy.

Reading the *Confession*, one gets the impression that Patrick's opponents were throwing a number of charges against him to see which would stick. In the fourth paragraph of the *Confession*, Patrick launched, almost without warning, into a full-blown creed. Had someone challenged his theological orthodoxy? He reassured the reader that he was as orthodox as could be:

For there is no other God, nor ever was before, nor shall be hereafter, but God the Father, unbegotten and without beginning, in whom all things began, whose are all things, as we have been taught; and his son Jesus Christ, who manifestly always existed with the Father, before the beginning of time in the spirit with the Father, indescribably begotten before all things, and all things visible and invisible were made by him. He was made man, conquered death and was received into Heaven, to the Father who gave him all power over every name in Heaven and on Earth and in Hell, so that every tongue should confess that Jesus Christ is Lord and God, in whom we believe. And we look to his imminent coming again, the judge of the living and the dead, who will render to each according to his deeds. And he poured out his Holy Spirit on us in abundance, the gift and pledge of immortality, which makes the believers and the obedient into sons of God and co-heirs of Christ who is revealed, and we worship one God in the Trinity of holy name.[13]

Patrick's methods were unorthodox. So was his attitude toward authority. His ideas about the barbarians went against the received orthodoxy of his day. But when it came to theology, he wanted to be sure his readers knew that he adhered to a strict Trinitarian orthodoxy.

Near the end of the *Confession*, Patrick launched into another theological discussion that seems a little out of place: "For the sun we see rises each day for us at [God's] command, but it will never reign, neither will its splendor last, but all who worship it will come wretchedly to punishment. We, on the other hand, shall not die, who believe in and worship the true sun, Christ, who will never die."[14]

Why did Patrick feel the need to take a stand against sun worship? His audience here was British clergymen. Surely he wasn't concerned about them lapsing into sun worship. Is it possible that Patrick has been accused of "going native" in Ireland, mixing in a little sun worship with his Christianity in order to make it appealing to the locals? Patrick's work would have seemed so foreign, so outlandish to his peers and his superiors in the British church that they might have believed all sorts of things about him and his methods. *If Patrick is not looking to make good Romans out of the Irish*, they might have been asking, *then what exactly is he doing?*

Patrick devoted quite a lot of time and effort to the question of money. In an earlier chapter we discussed the possibility that the British church that financed Patrick's work in Ireland might not have considered it a good use of their money. It appears that Patrick also was accused of using his position in Ireland to enrich himself. It is not hard to imagine the conversations of Patrick's accusers:

> *"Why on earth would anyone voluntarily go out among the Irish heathens?"*

> *"He must have some angle."*

"Maybe he's figured out some way to make money out there."

A charismatic leader, after all, does have plenty of opportunities to make money from his followers if he is unscrupulous. Patrick took care to prove that his hands were clean on this account.

Patrick called on his British brothers—men he had known for many years, since his training for the priesthood—to remember that he had always demonstrated integrity. "You know, as God does, how I went about among you from my youth in the faith of truth and in sincerity of heart."[15] Nothing has changed, he insisted. He had shown the same integrity among the heathen. "God knows I did not cheat any one of them, nor consider it, for the sake of God and his Church, lest I arouse them and [bring about] persecution for them and for all of us, and lest the Lord's name be blasphemed because of me."[16]

This is one area, said Patrick, in which even he—considering that he thought himself to be "ignorant in all things"—had sense enough to cover himself. Anytime any of his Irish converts gave him a gift or threw some little ornament on the altar for him, he always gave it back. "In the hope of eternity, I safeguarded myself in all things, so that they might not cheat me out of my office of service on any pretext of dishonesty, and so that I should not in the smallest way provide any occasion for defamation or disparagement on the part of unbelievers."[17] On the contrary, he said, he spent money rather than received it. We have already seen the large outlay that was required, bribing kings, paying bodyguards, paying off "those who were administering justice in those regions." (See chapter 5.)

No, Patrick insisted, there is no angle, no self-interest. And indeed, he had voluntarily enslaved himself to the people who had once enslaved him violently. "I testify in truthfulness and gladness of heart," he wrote, "before God and his holy angels that I never had any reason, except the Gospel and his promises, ever to have returned to that nation from which I had previously escaped with difficulty."[18]

No reason but the "Gospel." Jesus told his disciples, "Go into all the world and proclaim the gospel to the whole creation" (Mark 16:15 ESV). The widespread assumption in Patrick's time was that once the gospel had spread to the whole world, Christ would come back in glory. He would have no reason to wait any longer, the work of the gospel being finished. By Patrick's time, the gospel had indeed spread to the whole of what most Romans considered "the world." The Roman Empire was thoroughly Christian. That the gospel had not spread to kingdoms beyond the Roman Empire was no more interesting (and no more surprising) to them than it would be for a modern Christian to realize that the gospel hasn't spread among the animal kingdom.

Patrick had a bigger vision than that.

As you may recall from chapter 2, when he was first kidnapped and carried to Ireland, Patrick quoted the prophet who spoke of God punishing his people by scattering them to the ends of the earth. In his second sojourn in Ireland, however, that idea of "the ends of the earth" had a whole new meaning. It was the fulfillment of a promise: "I have made you a light for the Gentiles, that you may bring salvation to the ends of the earth" (Acts 13:47). That is the work that Patrick was about—bringing salvation to the uttermost "ends of the earth." In his mind, there was nothing metaphorical about that idea: again, he believed Ireland to be the very end of the inhabited world. To the west and to the north, he knew of no more people.

Patrick lived his whole life in the belief that he was living near the end of time. In his youth, watching the breakdown of Roman order, hearing his elders talk about how things weren't like they used to be, it wouldn't be hard to believe. Being snatched out of that world and into one that was even less civilized would have felt truly apocalyptic. In both of those contexts, the end would have seemed like something that was happening *to* him. In his missionary work in Ireland, Patrick believed himself to be bringing about the end of time and ushering in the kingdom of God.

In the middle of the *Confession*, Patrick strung together a series of biblical promises regarding the ends of the earth and the end of time. He quoted Jesus—"'Many shall come from east and west and shall sit at table with Abraham and Isaac and Jacob'"—then added, "Just as we believe that believers will come from all the world."[19] Again, Patrick was unusual among Roman Catholics of his era in believing that "all the world" meant there would be believers from the world *beyond* the Roman Empire.

Having taken the gospel across the western threshold of the empire, Patrick believed he had taken a major step toward bringing about the end of time. Quoting Jesus from Matthew 24:14, he wrote, "This Gospel of the Kingdom shall be preached throughout the whole world as a witness to all nations: and then the end of the world shall come."[20]

Here is one of the paradoxes of Patrick's character: he was a thoroughly humble man, yet he believed he was the very instrument by which God was completing human history. That, in the end, was Patrick's authority for this most unorthodox mission of his: his work represented the fulfillment of prophecy. Invoking Scripture again, he wrote:

> And in Hosea he says: "Those who are not my people I will call my people, and those not beloved I will call my beloved, and in the very place where it was said to them, You are not my people, they will be called 'Sons of the living God.'"
>
> So, how is it that in Ireland, where they never had any knowledge of God but, always, until now, cherished idols and unclean things, they are lately become a people of the Lord, and are called children of God?[21]

It is a beautiful vision for his people, the Irish people. They were not beloved, but they were *God's* beloved. They had been told—by the very people who claimed to speak for God—that they were not God's people, but now they were being called sons of the living God. Patrick marveled that he had been a part of such a reversal. It was the divine comedy at work again.

And no more likely than a leper sailing across the sea astride a stone altar.

EPILOGUE

Before the Irish, no people had ever submitted to the Christian gospel who had not first submitted to Roman rule. The Irish were a fierce people. They had never bowed to the yoke of a foreign ruler. Why, then, did they yield to a bishop?

One of the Patrick legends may give a clue. Patrick came upon two brothers whose quarrel over their inheritance had just turned into a swordfight. Moved by "pity of these unpitying men" (a most Patrician sentiment), Patrick froze the two brothers in mid-blow. Thus immobilized, the men had no choice but to listen to the gospel of peace as presented by the saint. Having heard his speech, the quarrelsome brothers "returned unto the mutual kindness of brotherly love," received Patrick's blessing, and together decided to build a church where once they had tried to kill one another.[1]

Ireland was a violent place, where brother fought brother— or, in any case, tribe fought neighboring tribe—as a way of life. Patrick brought to the Irish a whole new way of living, of seeing the world and their fellow men. He came wielding no earthly power. Such institutional authority as he had would

101

have meant nothing to the Irish. They paused long enough to listen—and they heard a gospel that made sense to them. They saw in Patrick's person—in his very presence among them—that forgiveness was possible, that hardship need not result in bitterness—and that the meek just might inherit the earth after all.

Appendix A

SAINT PATRICK'S WRITINGS

The Confession

1. I, Patrick, a sinner, a most simple countryman, the least of all the faithful and most contemptible to many, had for father the deacon Calpurnius, son of the late Potitus, a priest, of the settlement [vicus] of Bannavem Taburniae; he had a small villa nearby where I was taken captive. I was at that time about sixteen years of age. I did not, indeed, know the true God; and I was taken into captivity in Ireland with many thousands of people, according to our deserts, for quite drawn away from God, we did not keep his precepts, nor were we obedient to our priests who used to remind us of our salvation. And the Lord brought down on us the fury of his being and scattered us among many nations, even to the ends of the earth, where I, in my smallness, am now to be found among foreigners.

2. And there the Lord opened my mind to an awareness of my unbelief, in order that, even so late, I might remember my transgressions and turn with all my heart to the Lord my God, who had regard for my insignificance and pitied my youth and ignorance. And he watched over me before I knew him, and before I learned sense or even distinguished between good and evil, and he protected me, and consoled me as a father would his son.

3. Therefore, indeed, I cannot keep silent, nor would it be proper, so many favours and graces has the Lord deigned to bestow on me in the land of my captivity. For after chastisement from God, and recognizing him, our way to repay him is to exalt him and confess his wonders before every nation under heaven.

4. For there is no other God, nor ever was before, nor shall be hereafter, but God the Father, unbegotten and without beginning, in whom all things began, whose are all things, as we have been taught; and his son Jesus Christ, who manifestly always existed with the Father, before the beginning of time in the spirit with the Father, indescribably begotten before all things, and all things visible and invisible were made by him. He was made man, conquered death and was received into Heaven, to the Father who gave him all power over every name in Heaven and on Earth and in Hell, so that every tongue should confess that Jesus Christ is Lord and God, in whom we believe. And we look to his imminent coming again, the judge of the living and the dead, who will render to each according to his deeds. And

he poured out his Holy Spirit on us in abundance, the gift and pledge of immortality, which makes the believers and the obedient into sons of God and co-heirs of Christ who is revealed, and we worship one God in the Trinity of holy name.

5. He himself said through the prophet: 'Call upon me in the day of' trouble; I will deliver you, and you shall glorify me.' And again: 'It is right to reveal and publish abroad the works of God.'

6. I am imperfect in many things, nevertheless I want my brethren and kinsfolk to know my nature so that they may be able to perceive my soul's desire.

7. I am not ignorant of what is said of my Lord in the Psalm: 'You destroy those who speak a lie.' And again: 'A lying mouth deals death to the soul.' And likewise the Lord says in the Gospel: 'On the day of judgment men shall render account for every idle word they utter.'

8. So it is that I should mightily fear, with terror and trembling, this judgment on the day when no one shall be able to steal away or hide, but each and all shall render account for even our smallest sins before the judgment seat of Christ the Lord.

9. And therefore for some time I have thought of writing, but I have hesitated until now, for truly, I feared to expose myself to the criticism of men, because I have not studied like others, who have assimilated both Law and the Holy Scriptures equally and have never changed their idiom since their infancy, but instead were always learning it increasingly, to perfection, while my idiom and language have been translated into

a foreign tongue. So it is easy to prove from a sample of my writing, my ability in rhetoric and the extent of my preparation and knowledge, for as it is said, 'wisdom shall be recognized in speech, and in understanding, and in knowledge and in the learning of truth.'

10. But why make excuses close to the truth, especially when now I am presuming to try to grasp in my old age what I did not gain in my youth because my sins prevented me from making what I had read my own? But who will believe me, even though I should say it again? A young man, almost a beard-less boy, I was taken captive before I knew what I should desire and what I should shun. So, consequently, today I feel ashamed and I am mightily afraid to expose my ignorance, because, [not] eloquent, with a small vocabulary, I am unable to explain as the spirit is eager to do and as the soul and the mind indicate.

11. But had it been given to me as to others, in gratitude I should not have kept silent, and if it should appear that I put myself before others, with my ignorance and my slower speech, in truth, it is written: 'The tongue of the stammerers shall speak rapidly and distinctly.' How much harder must we try to attain it, we of whom it is said: 'You are an epistle of Christ in greet-ing to the ends of the earth . . . written on your hearts, not with ink but with the Spirit of the living God.' And again, the Spirit witnessed that the rustic life was created by the Most High.

12. I am, then, first of all, countryfied, an exile, evidently unlearned, one who is not able to see into the future, but I know for certain, that before I was humbled I was like a stone lying in

deep mire, and he that is mighty came and in his mercy raised me up and, indeed, lifted me high up and placed me on top of the wall. And from there I ought to shout out in gratitude to the Lord for his great favours in this world and for ever, that the mind of man cannot measure.

13. Therefore be amazed, you great and small who fear God, and you men of God, eloquent speakers, listen and contemplate. Who was it summoned me, a fool, from the midst of those who appear wise and learned in the law and powerful in rhetoric and in all things? Me, truly wretched in this world, he inspired before others that I could be—if I would—such a one who, with fear and reverence, and faithfully, without complaint, would come to the people to whom the love of Christ brought me and gave me in my lifetime, if I should be worthy, to serve them truly and with humility.

14. According, therefore, to the measure of one's faith in the Trinity, one should proceed without holding back from danger to make known the gift of God and everlasting consolation, to spread God's name everywhere with confidence and without fear, in order to leave behind, after my death, foundations for my brethren and sons whom I baptized in the Lord in so many thousands.

15. And I was not worthy, nor was I such that the Lord should grant his humble servant this, that after hardships and such great trials, after captivity, after many years, he should give me so much favour in these people, a thing which in the time of my youth I neither hoped for nor imagined.

16. But after I reached Ireland I used to pasture the flock each day and I used to pray many times a day. More and more did the love of God, and my fear of him and faith increase, and my spirit was moved so that in a day [I said] from one up to a hundred prayers, and in the night a like number; besides I used to stay out in the forests and on the mountain and I would wake up before daylight to pray in the snow, in icy coldness, in rain, and I used to feel neither ill nor any slothfulness, because, as I now see, the Spirit was burning in me at that time.

17. And it was there of course that one night in my sleep I heard a voice saying to me: 'You do well to fast: soon you will depart for your home country.' And again, a very short time later, there was a voice prophesying: 'Behold, your ship is ready.' And it was not close by, but, as it happened, two hundred miles away, where I had never been nor knew any person. And shortly thereafter I turned about and fled from the man with whom I had been for six years, and I came, by the power of God who directed my route to advantage (and I was afraid of nothing), until I reached that ship.

18. And on the same day that I arrived, the ship was setting out from the place, and I said that I had the wherewithal to sail with them; and the steersman was displeased and replied in anger, sharply: 'By no means attempt to go with us.' Hearing this I left them to go to the hut where I was staying, and on the way I began to pray, and before the prayer was finished I heard one of them shouting loudly after me: 'Come quickly because the men are calling you.' And immediately I went back to them

and they started to say to me: 'Come, because we are admitting you out of good faith; make friendship with us in any way you wish.' (And so, on that day, I refused to suck the breasts of these men from fear of God, but nevertheless I had hopes that they would come to faith in Jesus Christ, because they were barbarians.) And for this I continued with them, and forthwith we put to sea.

19. And after three days we reached land, and for twenty-eight days journeyed through uninhabited country, and the food ran out and hunger overtook them; and one day the steersman began saying: 'Why is it, Christian? You say your God is great and all-powerful; then why can you not pray for us? For we may perish of hunger; it is unlikely indeed that we shall ever see another human being.' In fact, I said to them, confidently: 'Be converted by faith with all your heart to my Lord God, because nothing is impossible for him, so that today he will send food for you on your road, until you be sated, because everywhere he abounds.' And with God's help this came to pass; and behold, a herd of swine appeared on the road before our eyes, and they slew many of them, and remained there for two nights, and the men were full of their meat and well restored, for many of them had fainted and would otherwise have been left half dead by the wayside. And after this they gave the utmost thanks to God, and I was esteemed in their eyes, and from that day they had food abundantly. They discovered wild honey, besides, and they offered a share to me, and one of them said: 'It is a sacrifice.' Thanks be to God, I tasted none of it.

20. The very same night while I was sleeping Satan attacked me violently, as I will remember as long as I shall be in this body; and there fell on top of me as it were, a huge rock, and not one of my members had any force. But from whence did it come to me, ignorant in the spirit, to call upon 'Helias'? And meanwhile I saw the sun rising in the sky, and while I was crying out 'Helias, Helias' with all my might, lo, the brilliance of that sun fell upon me and immediately shook me free of all the weight; and I believe that I was aided by Christ my Lord, and that his Spirit then was crying out for me, and I hope that it will be so in the day of my affliction, just as it says in the Gospel: 'In that hour', the Lord declares, 'it is not you who speaks but the Spirit of your Father speaking in you.'

21. And a second time, after many years, I was taken captive. On the first night I accordingly remained with my captors, but I heard a divine prophecy, saying to me: 'You shall be with them for two months.' So it happened. On the sixtieth night the Lord delivered me from their hands.

22. On the journey he provided us with food and fire and dry weather every day, until on the tenth day we came upon people. As I mentioned above, we had journeyed through an unpopulated country for twenty-eight days, and in fact the night that we came upon people we had no food.

23. And after a few years I was again in Britain with my parents [kinsfolk], and they welcomed me as a son, and asked me, in faith, that after the great tribulations I had endured I should not go anywhere else away from them. And, of course, there,

in a vision of the night, I saw a man whose name was Victoricus coming as if from Ireland with innumerable letters, and he gave me one of them, and I read the beginning of the letter: 'The Voice of the Irish'; and as I was reading the beginning of the letter I seemed at that moment to hear the voice of those who were beside the forest of Foclut which is near the western sea, and they were crying as if with one voice: 'We beg you, holy youth, that you shall come and shall walk again among us.' And I was stung intensely in my heart so that I could read no more, and thus I awoke. Thanks be to God, because after so many years the Lord bestowed on them according to their cry.

24. And another night—God knows, I do not, whether within me or beside me— . . . most words . . . which I heard and could not understand, except at the end of the speech it was represented thus: 'He who gave his life for you, he it is who speaks within you.' And thus I awoke, joyful.

25. And on a second occasion I saw Him praying within me, and I was as it were, inside my own body, and I heard Him above me—that is, above my inner self. He was praying powerfully with sighs. And in the course of this I was astonished and wondering, and I pondered who it could be who was praying within me. But at the end of the prayer it was revealed to me that it was the Spirit. And so I awoke and remembered the Apostle's words: 'Likewise the Spirit helps us in our weakness; for we know not how to pray as we ought. But the Spirit Himself intercedes for us with sighs too deep for utterance.' And again: 'The Lord our advocate intercedes for us.'

26. And then I was attacked by a goodly number of my elders, who [brought up] my sins against my arduous episcopate. That day in particular I was mightily upset, and might have fallen here and for ever; but the Lord generously spared me, a convert, and an alien, for his name's sake, and he came powerfully to my assistance in that state of being trampled down. I pray God that it shall not be held against them as a sin that I fell truly into disgrace and scandal.

27. They brought up against me after thirty years an occurrence I had confessed before becoming a deacon. On account of the anxiety in my sorrowful mind, I laid before my close friend what I had perpetrated on a day—nay, rather in one hour—in my boyhood because I was not yet proof against sin. God knows—I do not—whether I was fifteen years old at the time, and I did not then believe in the living God, nor had I believed, since my infancy; but I remained in death and unbelief until I was severely rebuked, and in truth I was humbled every day by hunger and nakedness.

28. On the other hand, I did not proceed to Ireland of my own accord until I was almost giving up, but through this I was corrected by the Lord, and he prepared me so that today I should be what was once far from me, in order that I should have the care of—or rather, I should be concerned for—the salvation of others, when at that time, still, I was only concerned for myself.

29. Therefore, on that day when I was rebuked, as I have just mentioned, I saw in a vision of the night a document before

my face, without honour, and meanwhile I heard a divine prophecy, saying to me: 'We have seen with displeasure the face of the chosen one divested of [his good] name.' And he did not say 'You have seen with displeasure', but 'We have seen with displeasure' (as if He included Himself). He said then: 'He who touches you, touches the apple of my eye.'

30. For that reason, I give thanks to him who strengthened me in all things, so that I should not be hindered in my setting out and also in my work which I was taught by Christ my Lord; but more, from that state of affairs I felt, within me, no little courage, and vindicated my faith before God and man.

31. Hence, therefore, I say boldly that my conscience is clear now and hereafter. God is my witness that I have not lied in these words to you.

32. But rather, I am grieved for my very close friend, that because of him we deserved to hear such a prophecy. The one to whom I entrusted my soul! And I found out from a goodly number of brethren, before the case was made in my defence (in which I did not take part, nor was I in Britain, nor was it pleaded by me), that in my absence he would fight in my behalf. Besides, he told me himself: 'See, the rank of bishop goes to you'—of which I was not worthy. But how did it come to him, shortly afterwards, to disgrace me publicly, in the presence of all, good and bad, because previously, gladly and of his own free will, he pardoned me, as did the Lord, who is greater than all?

33. I have said enough. But all the same, I ought not to conceal God's gift which he lavished on us in the land of my

captivity, for then I sought him resolutely, and I found him there, and he preserved me from all evils (as I believe) through the in-dwelling of his Spirit, which works in me to this day. Again, boldly, but God knows, if this had been made known to me by man, I might, perhaps, have kept silent for the love of Christ.

34. Thus I give untiring thanks to God who kept me faithful in the day of my temptation, so that today I may confidently offer my soul as a living sacrifice for Christ my Lord; who am I, Lord? or, rather, what is my calling? that you appeared to me in so great a divine quality, so that today among the barbarians I might constantly exalt and magnify your name in whatever place I should be, and not only in good fortune, but even in affliction? So that whatever befalls me, be it good or bad, I should accept it equally, and give thanks always to God who revealed to me that I might trust in him, implicitly and forever, and who will encourage me so that, ignorant, and in the last days, I may dare to undertake so devout and so wonderful a work; so that I might imitate one of those whom, once, long ago, the Lord already pre-ordained to be heralds of his Gospel to witness to all peoples to the ends of the earth. So are we seeing, and so it is fulfilled; behold, we are witnesses because the Gospel has been preached as far as the places beyond which no man lives.

35. But it is tedious to describe in detail all my labours one by one. I will tell briefly how most holy God frequently delivered me, from slavery, and from the twelve trials with which my soul was threatened, from man traps as well, and from things

I am not able to put into words. I would not cause offence to readers, but I have God as witness who knew all things even before they happened, that, though I was a poor, ignorant waif, still he gave me abundant warnings through divine prophecy.

36. Whence came to me this wisdom which was not my own, I who neither knew the number of days nor had knowledge of God? Whence came the so great and so healthful gift of knowing or rather loving God, though I should lose homeland and family?

37. And many gifts were offered to me with weeping and tears, and I offended them [the donors], and also went against the wishes of a good number of my elders; but guided by God, I neither agreed with them nor deferred to them, not by my own grace but by God who is victorious in me and withstands them all, so that I might come to the Irish people to preach the Gospel and endure insults from unbelievers; that I might hear scandal of my travels, and endure many persecutions to the extent of prison; and so that I might give up my free birthright for the advantage of others, and if I should be worthy, I am ready [to give] even my life without hesitation; and most willingly for His name. And I choose to devote it to him even unto death, if God grant it to me.

38. I am greatly God's debtor, because he granted me so much grace, that through me many people would be reborn in God, and soon after confirmed, and that clergy would be ordained everywhere for them, the masses lately come to belief, whom the Lord drew from the ends of the earth, just as he

once promised through his prophets: 'To you shall the nations come from the ends of the earth, and shall say, "Our fathers have inherited naught but lies, worthless things in which there is no profit."' And again: 'I have set you to be a light for the Gentiles that you may bring salvation to the uttermost ends of the earth.'

39. And I wish to wait then for his promise which is never unfulfilled, just as it is promised in the Gospel: 'Many shall come from east and west and shall sit at table with Abraham and Isaac and Jacob.' Just as we believe that believers will come from all the world,

40. So for that reason one should, in fact, fish well and diligently, just as the Lord foretells and teaches, saying, 'Follow me, and I will make you fishers of men,' and, again, through the prophets: '"Behold, I am sending forth many fishers and hunters," says the Lord,' et cetera. So it behoved us to spread our nets, that a vast multitude and throng might be caught for God, and so there might be clergy everywhere who baptized and exhorted a needy and desirous people. Just as the Lord says in the Gospel, admonishing and instructing: 'Go therefore and make disciples of all nations, baptizing them in the name of the Father and of the Son and of the Holy Spirit, teaching them to observe all that I have commanded you; and lo, I am with you always to the end of time.' And again he says: 'Go forth into the world and preach the Gospel to all creation. He who believes and is baptized shall be saved; but he who does not believe shall be condemned.' And again: 'This Gospel of the Kingdom shall

be preached throughout the whole world as a witness to all nations; and then the end of the world shall come.' And likewise the Lord foretells through the prophet: 'And it shall come to pass in the last days (sayeth the Lord) that I will pour out my spirit upon all flesh, and your sons and daughters shall prophesy, and your young men shall see visions and your old men shall dream dreams; yea, and on my menservants and my maidservants in those days I will pour out my Spirit and they shall prophesy.' And in Hosea he says: 'Those who are not my people I will call my people, and those not beloved I will call my beloved, and in the very place where it was said to them, "You are not my people," they will be called 'Sons of the living God.'"

41. So, how is it that in Ireland, where they never had any knowledge of God but, always, until now, cherished idols and unclean things, they are lately become a people of the Lord, and are called children of God; the sons of the Irish [Scotti] and the daughters of the chieftains are to be seen as monks and virgins of Christ.

42. And there was, besides, a most beautiful, blessed, native-born noble Irish [Scotta] woman of adult age whom I baptized; and a few days later she had reason to come to us to intimate that she had received a prophecy from a divine messenger [who] advised her that she should become a virgin of Christ and she would draw nearer to God. Thanks be to God, six days from then, opportunely and most eagerly, she took the course that all virgins of God take, not with their fathers' consent but enduring the persecutions and deceitful hindrances of their parents.

Notwithstanding that, their number increases, (we do not know the number of them that are so reborn) besides the widows, and those who practise self-denial. Those who are kept in slavery suffer the most. They endure terrors and constant threats, but the Lord has given grace to many of his handmaidens, for even though they are forbidden to do so, still they resolutely follow his example.

43. So it is that even if I should wish to separate from them in order to go to Britain, and most willingly was I prepared to go to my homeland and kinsfolk—and not only there, but as far as Gaul to visit the brethren there, so that I might see the faces of the holy ones of my Lord, God knows how strongly I desired this—I am bound by the Spirit, who witnessed to me that if I did so he would mark me out as guilty, and I fear to waste the labour that I began, and not I, but Christ the Lord, who commanded me to come to be with them for the rest of my life, if the Lord shall will it and shield me from every evil, so that I may not sin before him.

44. So I hope that I did as I ought, but I do not trust myself as long as I am in this mortal body, for he is strong who strives daily to turn me away from the faith and true holiness to which I aspire until the end of my life for Christ my Lord, but the hostile flesh is always dragging one down to death, that is, to unlawful attractions. And I know in part why I did not lead a perfect life like other believers, but I confess to my Lord and do not blush in his sight, because I am not lying; from the time when I came to know him in my youth, the love of God and

fear of him increased in me, and right up until now, by God's favour, I have kept the faith.

45. What is more, let anyone laugh and taunt if he so wishes. I am not keeping silent, nor am I hiding the signs and wonders that were shown to me by the Lord many years before they happened, [he] who knew everything, even before the beginning of time.

46. Thus, I should give thanks unceasingly to God, who frequently forgave my folly and my negligence, in more than one instance so as not to be violently angry with me, who am placed as his helper, and I did not easily assent to what had been revealed to me, as the Spirit was urging; and the Lord took pity on me thousands upon thousands of times, because he saw within me that I was prepared, but that I was ignorant of what to do in view of my situation; because many were trying to prevent this mission. They were talking among themselves behind my back, and saying: 'Why is this fellow throwing himself into danger among enemies who know not God?' Not from malice, but having no liking for it; likewise, as I myself can testify, they perceived my rusticity. And I was not quick to recognize the grace that was then in me; I now know that I should have done so earlier.

47. Now I have put it frankly to my brethren and co-workers, who have believed me because of what I have foretold and still foretell to strengthen and reinforce your faith. I wish only that you, too, would make greater and better efforts. This will be my pride, for 'a wise son makes a proud father'.

48. You know, as God does, how I went about among you from my youth in the faith of truth and in sincerity of heart. As well as to the heathen among whom I live, I have shown them trust and always show them trust. God knows I did not cheat any one of them, nor consider it, for the sake of God and his Church, lest I arouse them and [bring about] persecution for them and for all of us, and lest the Lord's name be blasphemed because of me, for it is written: 'Woe to the men through whom the name of the Lord is blasphemed.'

49. For even though I am ignorant in all things, nevertheless I attempted to safeguard some and myself also. And I gave back again to my Christian brethren and the virgins of Christ and the holy women the small unasked for gifts that they used to give me or some of their ornaments which they used to throw on the altar. And they would be offended with me because I did this. But in the hope of eternity, I safeguarded myself carefully in all things, so that they might not cheat me of my office of service on any pretext of dishonesty, and so that I should not in the smallest way provide any occasion for defamation or disparagement on the part of unbelievers.

50. What is more, when I baptized so many thousands of people, did I hope for even half a jot from any of them? [If so] Tell me, and I will give it back to you. And when the Lord ordained clergy everywhere by my humble means, and I freely conferred office on them, if I asked any of them anywhere even for the price of one shoe, say so to my face and I will give it back.

51. More, I spent for you so that they would receive me. And I went about among you, and everywhere for your sake, in danger, and as far as the outermost regions beyond which no one lived, and where no one had ever penetrated before, to baptize or to ordain clergy or to confirm people. Conscientiously and gladly I did all this work by God's gift for your salvation.

52. From time to time I gave rewards to the kings, as well as making payments to their sons who travel with me; notwithstanding which, they seized me with my companions, and that day most avidly desired to kill me. But my time had not yet come. They plundered everything they found on us anyway, and fettered me in irons; and on the fourteenth day the Lord freed me from their power, and whatever they had of ours was given back to us for the sake of God on account of the indispensable friends whom we had made before.

53. Also you know from experience how much I was paying to those who were administering justice in all the regions, which I visited often. I estimate truly that I distributed to them not less than the price of fifteen men, in order that you should enjoy my company and I enjoy yours, always, in God. I do not regret this nor do I regard it as enough. I am paying out still and I shall pay out more. The Lord has the power to grant me that I may soon spend my own self, for your souls.

54. Behold, I call on God as my witness upon my soul that I am not lying; nor would I write to you for it to be an occasion for flattery or selfishness, nor hoping for honour from any one of you. Sufficient is the honour which is not yet seen, but in

which the heart has confidence. He who made the promise is faithful; he never lies.

55. But I see that even here and now, I have been exalted beyond measure by the Lord, and I was not worthy that he should grant me this, while I know most certainly that poverty and failure suit me better than wealth and delight (but Christ the Lord was poor for our sakes; I certainly am wretched and unfortunate; even if I wanted wealth I have no resources, nor is it my own estimation of myself, for daily I expect to be murdered or betrayed or reduced to slavery if the occasion arises. But I fear nothing, because of the promises of Heaven; for I have cast myself into the hands of Almighty God, who reigns everywhere. As the prophet says: 'Cast your burden on the Lord and he will sustain you.'

56. Behold now I commend my soul to God who is most faithful and for whom I perform my mission in obscurity, but he is no respecter of persons and he chose me for this service that I might be one of the least of his ministers.

57. For which reason I should make return for all that he returns me. But what should I say, or what should I promise to my Lord, for I, alone, can do nothing unless he himself vouchsafe it to me. But let him search my heart and [my] nature, for I crave enough for it, even too much, and I am ready for him to grant me that I drink of his chalice, as he has granted to others who love him.

58. Therefore may it never befall me to be separated by my God from his people whom he has won in this most remote

land. I pray God that he gives me perseverance, and that he will deign that I should be a faithful witness for his sake right up to the time of my passing.

59. And if at any time I managed anything of good for the sake of my God whom I love, I beg of him that he grant it to me to shed my blood for his name with proselytes and captives, even should I be left unburied, or even were my wretched body to be torn limb from limb by dogs or savage beasts, or were it to be devoured by the birds of the air, I think, most surely, were this to have happened to me, I had saved both my soul and my body. For beyond any doubt on that day we shall rise again in the brightness of the sun, that is, in the glory of Christ Jesus our Redeemer, as children of the living God and co-heirs of Christ, made in his image; for we shall reign through him and for him and in him.

60. For the sun we see rises each day for us at [his] command, but it will never reign, neither will its splendour last, but all who worship it will come wretchedly to punishment. We, on the other hand, shall not die, who believe in and worship the true sun, Christ, who will never die, no more shall he die who has done Christ's will, but will abide for ever just as Christ abides for ever, who reigns with God the Father Almighty and with the Holy Spirit before the beginning of time and now and for ever and ever. Amen.

61. Behold over and over again I would briefly set out the words of my confession. I testify in truthfulness and gladness of heart before God and his holy angels that I never had

any reason, except the Gospel and his promises, ever to have returned to that nation from which I had previously escaped with difficulty.

62. But I entreat those who believe in and fear God, whoever deigns to examine or receive this document composed by the obviously unlearned sinner Patrick in Ireland, that nobody shall ever ascribe to my ignorance any trivial thing that I achieved or may have expounded that was pleasing to God, but accept and truly believe that it would have been the gift of God. And this is my confession before I die.

This translation of *The Confession of St. Patrick* is from http://www.ccel.org/ccel/patrick/confession.txt, and is public domain. Inconsistencies in punctuation, grammar, and spellings are true to the original text.

Appendix B

ST. PATRICK'S WRITINGS

The Letter

1. Patrick the sinner, unlearned verily:—I confess that I am a bishop, appointed by God, in Ireland. Most surely I deem that from God I have received what I am. And so I dwell in the midst of barbarians, a stranger and an exile for the love of God. He is witness if this is so. Not that I desired to utter from my mouth anything so harshly and so roughly; but I am compelled *by zeal for God* (Rom. x. 2); and *the truth of Christ* (2 Cor. xi. 10) roused me, for the love of my nearest friends and sons, for whom I have *not regarded* my fatherland and kindred, yea nor my *life, even unto death* (Phil. ii. 30), if I am worthy. I have vowed to my God to teach the heathen, though I be despised by some.

2. With mine own hand have I written and composed

these words to be given and delivered and sent to the soldiers of Coroticus—I do not say to my fellow-citizens or to the fellow-citizens of the holy Romans, but to those who are fellow-citizens of demons because of their evil deeds. Behaving like enemies, they are dead while they live, allies of the Scots and apostate Picts, as though wishing to gorge themselves with blood, the blood of innocent Christians, whom I in countless numbers begot to God and confirmed in Christ.

3. On the day following that on which the newly baptized, in white array, were anointed—it was still fragrant on their foreheads while they were cruelly butchered and slaughtered with the sword by the aforesaid persons—I sent a letter with a holy presbyter whom I had taught from his infancy, clergy accompanying him, with a request that they would grant us some of the booty and of the baptized captives whom they had taken. They jeered at them.

4. Therefore I know not what I should the rather mourn: whether those who are slain, or those whom they captured, or those whom the devil grievously ensnared. In everlasting punishment they will become slaves of hell along with him; for verily *whosoever committeth sin is a bondservant of sin* (John viii. 34), and is called *a son of the devil* (Acts xiii.10).

5. On this account let every man that feareth God learn that aliens they are from me and from, Christ my God, *for whom I am an ambassador* (Eph. vi. 20)—patricide, fratricide as he is!— *ravening wolves* (Acts xx. 29) *eating up the people* of the Lord *as it were bread* (Ps. xiv. 4). As he saith, *O Lord, the ungodly have*

destroyed thy law (Ps. cxix. 126), which in the last times he had excellently [and] kindly planted in Ireland; and it was builded by the favour of God.

6. I make no false claim. I have part with those whom *he called and predestinated* (Rom. viii. 30) to preach the Gospel amidst no small persecutions, *even unto the ends of the earth* (Acts xiii. 47), even though the enemy casts an evil eye on me by means of the tyranny of Coroticus, who fears neither God nor his priests whom he chose, and to whom he granted that highest, divine, sublime power, that *whom they should bind on earth should be bound in heaven* (Matt. xvi. 19).

7. Whence therefore, *ye holy and humble men of heart* (Dan. iii. 87), I beseech you very much. It is not right to pay court to such men, nor to take food or drink with them; nor ought one to accept their almsgivings, until [doing] sore penance with shedding of tears, they make amends to God, and liberate the servants of God and the baptized handmaidens of Christ, for whom he died and was crucified.

8. *The most High approveth not the gifts of the wicked. He that offereth sacrifice of the goods of the poor is as one that sacrificeth the son in the presence of his father?* (Ecclus. xxxiv. 23, 24). *The riches*, he saith, *which he hath gathered unjustly will be vomited up from his belly. The angel of death draggeth him away. He will be tormented by the fury of dragons. The viper's tongue shall slay him; unquenchable fire devoureth him* (Job xx. 15, 16).

And therefore, *Woe to those who fill themselves with what is not their own* (Hab. ii. 6). And, *What is a man profited, if he shall gain the whole world, and lose his own soul?* (Matt. xvi. 26).

9. It would be tedious to discuss or declare [their deeds] one by one, [and] to gather from the whole law testimonies concerning such greed. Avarice is a deadly sin; *Thou shall not covet thy neighbour's goods; Thou shalt do no murder* (Rom. xiii. 9); *A murderer cannot be with Christ; He that hateth his brother is reckoned as a murderer.* And again, *He that loveth not his brother abideth in death* (1 John iii. 14, 15). How much more guilty is he that hath stained his hands with the blood of the sons of God whom he recently purchased in the ends of the earth through the exhortation of our littleness.

10. Was it without God, or according to the flesh, that I came to Ireland? Who compelled me? *I am bound in the Spirit* (Acts. xx. 22) not to see any one of my kinsfolk. Is it from me that springs that godly compassion which I exercise towards that nation who once took me captive, and made havoc of the menservants and maidservants of my father's house? I was freeborn according to the flesh; I am born of a father who was a decurion; but I sold my noble rank—I blush not to state it, nor am I sorry—for the profit of others; in short, I am a slave in Christ to a foreign nation for the unspeakable glory of the *eternal life which is in Christ Jesus our Lord* (Rom. vi. 23).

11. And if my own know me not, *a prophet hath no honour in his own country* (John iv. 44). Perchance we are not of *the one fold* (John x. 16), nor have *one God and Father* (Eph. iv. 6; Mal. ii. 10). As he saith, *He that is not with me is against me, and*

he that gathereth not with me scattereth abroad (Matt. xii. 30). It is not meet that *one pulleth down and another buildeth up* (Ecclus. xxxiv. 28). *I seek not mine own* (1 Cor. xiii. 5).

It was not any grace in me, but God that *put this earnest care into my heart* (2 Cor. viii. 16), that I should be one of the *hunters* or *fishers* (Jer. xvi. 16) whom long ago God foreshowed would come *in the last days* (Acts ii. 17).

12. Men look askance at me. What shall I do, O Lord? I am exceedingly despised. Lo, around me are thy sheep torn to pieces and spoiled, and that too by the robbers aforesaid, by the orders of Coroticus with hostile disposition.

Far from the love of God is he who betrays Christians into the hands of the Scots and Picts. *Ravening wolves* (Acts xx. 29) have swallowed up the flock of the Lord which verily in Ireland was growing up excellently with the greatest care. And the sons and daughters of Scottic chieftains who were monks and virgins of Christ I cannot reckon. Wherefore, *be not pleased with the wrong done to the just; even unto hell it shall not please thee* (Ecclus. ix. 17).

13. Which of the saints would not shudder to jest and feast with such men? They have filled their houses with the spoil of dead Christians. They live by plunder. Wretched men, they know not that it is poison; they offer the deadly food to their friends and sons; just as Eve did not understand that verily it was death that she handed to her husband. So are all they who do wrong; they work death as their eternal punishment.

14. This is the custom of the Roman Gauls:—They send

holy and fit men to the Franks and other heathen with many thousands of *solidi* to redeem baptized captives. Thou rather slayest and sellest them to a foreign *nation which knows not God* (1 Thess. iv. 5). Thou handest over *the members of Christ* (1 Cor. vi. 15) as it were to a brothel. What manner of hope in God hast thou, or has he who consents with thee, or who holds converse with thee in words of flattery? God will judge; for it is written, *Not only those who commit evil, but those that consent with them shall be damned* (Rom. i. 32).

15. I know not *what I should say, or what I should speak* (John xii. 49) further about the departed ones of the sons of God, whom the sword has touched roughly above measure. For it is written, *Weep with them that weep* (Rom. xii. 15), and again, *If one member suffer, let all the members suffer with it* (I Cor. xii. 26). On this account the Church bewails and laments her sons and daughters whom the sword has not as yet slain, but who are banished and carried off to distant lands where sin openly, grievously, and shamelessly abounds. There freemen are put up for sale, Christians are reduced to slavery, and, worst of all, to most degraded, most vile and apostate Picts.

16. Therefore in sadness and grief shall I cry aloud : O most lovely and beloved brethen, and sons whom *I begot in Christ* (1 Cor. iv. 15)—I cannot reckon them—what shall I do for you? I am not worthy to come to the aid of either God or men. *The wickedness of the wicked hath prevailed against us* (Ps. lxv. 3). *We are become* as it were *strangers* (Ps. lxix. 8). Perchance they do not believe that we receive *one baptism*, and that we have *one*

God and Father (Eph. iv. 5). It is in their eyes a disgraceful thing that we were born in Ireland. As he saith, *Have ye not one God? Why do ye, each one, forsake his neighbour?* (Mal. ii. 10).

17. Therefore, I grieve for you, I grieve, O ye most dear to me. But again, I rejoice within myself. *I have not laboured* for nought, and my going abroad was not *in vain* (Phil. ii. 16). And there happened a crime so horrid and unspeakable! Thanks be to God, it was as baptized believers that ye departed from the world to Paradise. I can see you. Ye have begun to remove to where *there shall be no night nor sorrow nor death any more* (Rev. xxii. 5; xxi. 4); but *ye shall leap like calves loosened from their bands, and ye shall tread down the wicked, and they shall be ashes under your feet* (Mal. iv. 2, 3).

18. Ye therefore shall reign with apostles and prophets and martyrs. Ye shall take everlasting kingdoms, -as he himself witnesseth, saying, *They shall come from the east and west, and shall sit down with Abraham and Isaac and Jacob in the kingdom of heaven* (Matt. viii. 11). *Without are dogs and sorcerers and murderers;* and *liars and false swearers shall have their part in the lake of everlasting fire* (Rev. xxii. 15; xxi. 8). Not without just cause the apostle saith, *Where the righteous shall scarcely be saved, where shall the sinner and the ungodly transgressor of the law recognize himself?* (1 Pet. iv. 18).

19. Wherefore then, where shall Coroticus with his accursed followers, rebels against Christ, where shall they see themselves?—they who distribute baptized damsels as rewards, and that for the sake of a wretched temporal kingdom, which

verily passes away in a moment like a cloud or *smoke which is verily dispersed by the wind* (Wisd. v. 15). *So shall the* deceitful *wicked perish at the presence of the Lord; but let the righteous feast* (Ps. lxviii. 2, 3) in great constancy with Christ. *They shall judge nations, and rule* (Wisd. iii. 8) over ungodly kings for ever and ever. Amen.

This translation of *Epistola ad Coroticum*, or *The Letter sent to the soldiers of Coroticus*, is from Newport J. D. White, *St. Patrick: His Writings and Life*, ed., Eleanor Hull, from series 5 (Lives of the Celtic Saints) of the Translations of Christian Literature series, and is in the public domain.

NOTES

Introduction

1. Jocelin (12th century–1199), *The Life and Acts of St. Patrick*, trans. Edmund L. Swift (public domain), chap. 27.
2. Aubrey de Vere, *The Legends of Saint Patrick* (public domain).
3. Jocelin, *The Life and Acts of St. Patrick*, chap. 149.
4. Ibid., chap. 124.
5. Ibid., chap. 148.
6. Ibid., chap. 81.
7. Patrick, *Confession* (public domain), part 6. See appendix for the full text of the *Confession*.
8. Thomas Cahill, *How the Irish Saved Civilization* (New York: Anchor, 1995), 122.

Chapter 1

1. Graham Thomas, "The Romans at Woodchester" from *A History of Woodchester and Selsley*, http://www.grahamthomas.com/history4.html.
2. Christopher A. Snyder, *An Age of Tyrants* (University Park, PA: Penn State University Press, 1998), 24.
3. Michael E. Jones, *The End of Roman Britain* (Ithaca, NY: Cornell University Press, 1998), 249.
4. Ibid., 250.
5. Jocelin, *The Life and Acts of St. Patrick*, chap. 5.
6. Ibid., chap. 8.
7. Patrick, *Confession*, part 1.
8. Ibid., part 27.
9. Maire B. de Paor, *Patrick: Pilgrim Apostle of Ireland* (William Morrow, 2002), 26.

10. Peter Salway, *The Roman Era: The British Isles: 55 BC–AD 410 (Short Oxford History of the British Isles)*, illustr. ed. (New York: Oxford University Press, 2002), 94. Salway notes three buildings that are "architecturally suitable for church use," but they could just as easily have been used for other purposes.

11. E. A. Thompson, *Who Was Saint Patrick?* (Suffolk, UK: Boydell, 1985; Rochester: Boydell, repr. 1999), 3–4. Citations are to the 1999 edition.

12. Cahill, *How the Irish Saved Civilization*, 60.

13. Patrick, *Confession*, part 27.

Chapter 2

1. Philip Freeman, *Ireland and the Classical World* (Austin: University of Texas Press, 2001), 49.

2. Ibid., 46.

3. Ibid., 44.

4. Ibid., 99.

5. Ibid.

6. Philip Freeman, *War, Women, and Druids* (Austin: University of Texas Press, 2002), 11.

7. Ibid., 26.

8. Maire B. de Paor, *Patrick*, 30.

9. Freeman, *War, Women, and Druids*, 46.

10. Ibid.

11. Jeffrey Gantz, transl., *Irish Myths and Sagas* (New York: Penguin Books, 1981), 127–29.

12. Liam de Paor, *Saint Patrick's World: The Christian Culture of Ireland's Apostolic Age* (Dublin: Four Courts Press, 1993; US: University of Notre Dame Press, 1997), 27.

13. Patrick, *Confession*, part 1.

14. Ibid.

15. Liam de Paor, *Saint Patrick's World*, 100. See also Wikipedia, s.v. "Saint Patrick," under the heading "In his own words," http://en.wikipedia.org/wiki/Saint_Patrick.

16. Patrick, *Confession*, part 2.

17. Ibid., part 16.

18. Ibid.
19. Eugene Peterson, *Leap Over a Wall: Earthy Spirituality for Everyday Christians* (New York: HarperCollins, 1997), 39–40.

CHAPTER 3

1. Patrick, *Confession*, part 17.
2. Jocelin, *The Life and Acts of St. Patrick*, chap. 16.
3. Ibid.
4. Ibid.
5. Liam de Paor, *Saint Patrick's World*, 23.
6. Patrick, *Confession*, part 16.
7. Ibid., part 18.
8. Ibid.
9. Ibid.
10. Philip Freeman, *St. Patrick of Ireland: A Biography* (New York: Simon & Schuster, 2004), 38.
11. Patrick, *Confession*, part 18.
12. Ibid., part 19.
13. Thompson, *Who Was Saint Patrick?* 30–34.
14. Patrick, *Confession*, part 19.
15. Ibid.
16. Ibid.
17. Ibid.
18. Ibid., part 20.
19. Ibid.
20. Ibid., part 60.
21. Ibid., part 20.
22. Patrick, "Saint Patrick's Breastplate," from Order of Saint Patrick, "Breastplate of St. Patrick," stanza 8, http://orderofsaintpatrick.org/breastplate.htm.
23. Patrick, *Confession*, part 21.
24. Jocelin, *The Life and Acts of St. Patrick*, chap. 20.

CHAPTER 4

1. Patrick, *Confession*, part 23.
2. Ibid.

3. Ibid.

4. Ibid., part 24. The use of the word *learned* comes from Maire B. de Paor's *Patrick: Pilgrim Apostle of Ireland*.

5. Ibid., parts 24–25.

6. Ibid., part 20.

7. Patrick, *St. Patrick's Epistle to the Christian Subjects of the Tyrant Coroticus*, in *The Most Ancient Lives of Saint Patrick*, ed. James O'Leary (public domain).

8. Patrick, *Confession*, part 1.

9. Ibid., part 9.

10. Ibid.

11. Ibid.

12. Thompson, *Who Was Saint Patrick?* 44.

13. Patrick, *Confession*, part 10.

14. Ibid., part 11.

15. Ibid., part 13.

16. Jocelin, *The Life and Acts of St. Patrick*, chap. 23.

17. Liam de Paor, *Saint Patrick's World*, 79.

18. Ibid.

19. Ibid., 179.

20. Patrick, *Confession*, part 26.

21. Ibid., part 27.

22. Ibid.

23. Ibid., part 32.

24. Ibid., part 26.

25. Ibid., part 29.

26. Ibid., part 26.

27. Ibid., part 32.

CHAPTER 5

1. Liam de Paor, *Saint Patrick's World*, 180.

2. Ibid.

3. Jocelin, *The Life and Acts of St. Patrick*, chap. 32.

4. MacEvin, *The Tripartite Life*, part 1, in *The Most Ancient Lives of Saint Patrick*, ed. James O'Leary (public domain).

5. Ibid.

6. Ibid.

7. Patrick, *Confession*, part 35.

8. Patrick, *A Letter to the Soldiers of Coroticus*, part 3, para.10, in *The Confession of Saint Patrick and Letter to Coroticus*, transl. John Skinner with a foreword by John O'Donohue (New York: Image, 1998), 7.

9. Patrick, *Confession*, part 37.

10. Ibid.

11. Ibid., part 38.

12. Ibid., part 50.

13. Ibid., part 51.

14. Ibid., part 52.

15. Ibid.

16. Ibid., part 53.

17. E. A. Thompson examined this question at considerable length in *Who Was Saint Patrick?* and though he arrived at few answers, the questions he raised are fascinating.

18. *Letter*, part 3, para. 10, from Skinner, *Confession and Letter*, 8.

19. Patrick, *Confession*, part 41.

20. Liam de Paor, *Saint Patrick's World*, 35.

21. Patrick, *Confession*, part 42.

22. Jocelin, *The Life and Acts of St. Patrick*, chap. 79.

23. Liam de Paor, *Saint Patrick's World*, 187.

24. Patrick, *Confession*, part 42.

25. Ibid., part 15.

26. Ibid., part 48.

27. Ibid., part 58.

28. Liam de Paor, *Saint Patrick's Life*, 191–92.

29. Ibid., part 55.

Chapter 6

1. *Letter*, part 1, para. 3, from Skinner, *Confession and Letter*, 3.

2. O'Leary, *Epistle*.

3. Ibid.

4. *Letter*, part 1, para. 1, from Skinner, *Confession and Letter*, 1.

5. O'Leary, *Epistle*.

6. *Letter*, part 1, para. 2, from Skinner, *Confession and Letter*, 2.

7. O'Leary, *Epistle*.

8. Ibid.

9. Ibid.

10. Ibid.

11. Ibid.

12. *Letter*, part 1, para. 5, from Skinner, *Confession and Letter*, 4.

13. Ibid., part 2, para. 6, p. 4

14. O'Leary, *Epistle*.

15. Ibid.

16. Ibid.

17. *Letter*, part 2, para. 8, from Skinner, *Confession and Letter*, 6.

18. O'Leary, *Epistle*.

19. Ibid.

20. Ibid.

21. *Letter*, part 3, para. 14, from Skinner, *Confession and Letter*, 11.

22. O'Leary, *Epistle*.

23. Ibid.

24. Ibid.

25. *Letter*, part 3, para. 20, from Skinner, *Confession and Letter*, 15.

CHAPTER 7

1. According to tradition, the apostle Thomas—Doubting Thomas— took the gospel as far as India. There is no historical evidence to prove (or disprove) that Thomas made the trip. The idea may have originated in the apocryphal Acts of Thomas, a third-century Gnostic work. In any case, in the sixteenth century, the "first" Catholic missionaries to India were surprised to find a long-established community of Christians already there—Christians who traced their spiritual lineage through Thomas.

2. In Paul's writings, the word *barbarians* appears exactly once, in Colossians 3:11—"Here there is no Greek or Jew, circumcised or uncircumcised, barbarian, Scythian, slave or free, but Christ is all, and is in all." In the book of Acts, when Paul's ship wrecks off the coast of Malta, the writer refers to the locals as "barbarians" (28:4 KJV). Malta, however, was part of the Roman Empire.

3. Peter Brown, *The World of Late Antiquity* (London: Thames &

Hudson, Ltd., 1971; New York: W. W. Norton, 1989; citations are to the Norton edition).

4. Ibid., 102.

5. Ibid., 112.

6. Ibid., 84.

7. Ibid.

8. Ibid., 87.

9. Ibid., 112.

10. Patrick, *Confession*, part 46.

11. Ibid., part 47.

12. Ibid.

13. Ibid., part 4.

14. Ibid., part 60.

15. Ibid., part 48.

16. Ibid.

17. Ibid., part 49.

18. Ibid., part 61.

19. Ibid., part 39.

20. Ibid., part 40.

21. Ibid., parts 40–41.

EPILOGUE

1. Jocelin, *The Life and Acts of St. Patrick*, chap. 76.

ACKNOWLEDGMENTS

This book was Joel Miller's idea before it was mine. Joel, here's hoping that your vision for the Christian Encounters series carries the day and makes Church history more accessible to a wider audience of readers.

John Eames of Eames Literary Services has been more than an agent; he has been a source of help and encouragement on this project from start to finish.

In the process of writing this book, I have depended even more than usual on the support and prayers of friends, who have been generous with both. Many thanks to my Thursday morning group: Jeff Gaw, Kevin Moore, Scott Holmes, Kevin Hamilton, Kolin Holladay, Jim Lyday, Jim Madrigal, Jon Selinger, and Steve Singleton.

Particular thanks goes to Brett and Laura Parks, who provided me with a quiet (eerily quiet!) place to finish this book, far from civilization's buzz and rattle. If it weren't for that time at your cabin, I might still be writing.

And as always, my deepest thanks are reserved for my wife, Lou Alice, who bears the greatest part of the burden when I'm finishing a book. You're a treasure beyond counting.

ABOUT THE AUTHOR

Jonathan Rogers' interest in Patrick began when his children came home from history class telling stories of the saint. Jonathan holds a Ph.D. in 17th century literature from Vanderbilt University.

The CHRISTIAN ENCOUNTERS series

Christian Encounters

JOHANN
SEBASTIAN
BACH
RICK MARSCHALL

WILLIAM F.
BUCKLEY
JEREMY LOTT

ST. FRANCIS
ROBERT WEST

ANNE
BRADSTREET
D.B. KELLOGG

J. R. R.
TOLKIE
MARK HORNE

Coming
August
2010

THOMAS NELSON
Since 1798